GOOD NEWS FOR WEARY WOMEN

Good news
-- for --
WEARY WOMEN

Escaping the bondage of
to-do lists, steps, and bad advice

ELYSE M. FITZPATRICK

Tyndale House Publishers, Inc.
Carol Stream, Illinois

Visit Tyndale online at www.tyndale.com.

Visit the author's website at www.elysefitzpatrick.com.

TYNDALE and Tyndale's quill logo are registered trademarks of Tyndale House Publishers, Inc.

Good News for Weary Women: Escaping the Bondage of To-Do Lists, Steps, and Bad Advice

Designed by Jacqueline L. Nuñez

Edited by Stephanie Rische

Published in association with Resurgence Publishing Inc., 1411 NW 50th St., Seattle, WA 98107.

Library of Congress Cataloging-in-Publication Data

Fitzpatrick, Elyse, date.
    Good news for weary women : escaping the bondage of to-do lists, steps, and bad advice / Elyse Fitzpatrick.
        pages cm. — (Resurgence books)
    Includes bibliographical references.
    ISBN 978-1-4143-9538-8 (sc)
1. Christian women—Religious life. 2. Time management—Religious aspects—Christianity. 3. Simplicity—Religious aspects—Christianity. I. Title.
  BV4527.F584 2014
  248.8'43—dc23   2014020742

Printed in the United States of America

20	19	18	17	16	15	14
7	6	5	4	3	2	1

To all the wearied, burdened, wounded, and struggling women who love their Lord but can't seem to find the joy, peace, or freedom they've heard so much about. Hear His good word for you: "Come to me, all who labor and are heavy laden, and I will give you rest" (Matthew 11:28).

CONTENTS

AUTHOR'S NOTE

IT'S MY HOPE that this book will be the catalyst for many discussions among women—whether over the phone, over coffee, in the park, or in small groups. It is also my hope that through these conversations, women will begin to open up about the ways they struggle to fulfill all the demands that are foisted upon them and that they will grow in their discernment—not only about the demands themselves but also about their own desire for approval as they check off all the little boxes on their list.

In all of this, I pray most sincerely that women will rediscover the profound grace that is ours through the good news: that we are forgiven, loved, and already counted perfect.

To help facilitate discussions, I have included questions at the end of each chapter. Feel free to use these questions in whatever way works best for you. For instance, you may want to look over them before reading the chapter so you'll have a sense of where the chapter is going. Or you may want to wait until the end and then go back through the chapter, underlining and reflecting on the important points. Or you're welcome to ignore them altogether, if you like.

The final question for each chapter asks for a summary of what you've read. This is something I do myself, because it's way too easy for me to forget what I've read, and then two years later, I wonder what the book was about . . . or whether I actually read it. Again, do this if you'd like to and if you find it helpful, but don't stress over it. Enjoy.

VOICES CRYING IN THE WILDERNESS

MY HEART ACHES for all the weary women who are desperate for good news. My heart aches because I've personally spoken to countless women who are burdened and exhausted and on the verge of either giving up on what has been passed off as Christianity or are nearly killing themselves trying to keep up with impossible demands. I've wept with women who are shocked by the freedom and grace of the gospel message—women who have trouble believing it, who can't get over thinking that God is mad at them.

I've watched women sigh in relief when I tell them that God can't be disappointed with them because disappointment is a by-product of unmet expectations and that God has none when it comes to them. I've had friends who have cut, burned, or starved themselves because they can't take the pain of their failure anymore, and they simply don't have the faith to keep trying to be good enough. Did it hurt when they pressed the cigarettes into their arms? Of course it did.

But this was nothing compared to the pain in their souls when they failed to measure up once again.

I've had other friends who didn't do anything so drastic but suffered silently for years, weighed down by burdens and expectations they could never measure up to.

I've wept with women who have spent their whole lives worshiping their family, only to lose their husband to pornography or adultery and their children to rebellion or atheism. These things are happening all around us. They are happening in our churches; they are happening in the lives of the women we see on Sundays. They may be happening in your life too. Maybe you long to believe that God really loves you but you think there must be a catch. Maybe you've been a Christian for twenty years but all you hear about is rules, not good news.

I have a daughter, two daughters-in-law, and two granddaughters, and if there is anything I want them to know, it is this:

> There is good news for you. You don't need to learn secret steps, try harder and harder, wear yourself out in an attempt to be beautiful, snag Mr. Perfect, or raise perfect children. You are already welcomed, loved, forgiven, and completely okay. You can laugh and rest and resist all the ways the world lies to you and tells you you're not good enough. And you can love God because He has already loved you. You can be free to fail, to rest, to love, to be weak, to grow, and to know that everything is already given to you in Him.

I've watched little girls who are told that their worth lies in their cuteness, in their ability to be a princess, in their being surrounded by all the right other little girls; and my heart breaks, because no one can maintain princess status her whole life. And I've cried for other little girls, whose moms didn't buy them tutus to wear to school, whose teeth aren't always gleaming, who would rather dig in the dirt than play with babies, who are shunned and teased, because I wonder if their lives will be marked by love and welcome or if they will always think that they don't quite fit in.

I've watched teen girls who define themselves solely by their friends and their looks and their worth in the eyes of guys, and I've feared that they will humiliate themselves to try to earn some guy's benediction . . . only to discover that it is not the same thing as love. And I've seen ungainly girls who hide behind food or drugs or self-harm only to discover that when they're seeking human approval, the emptiness never ends.

I've talked to women who are completely heartbroken because their daughters—the girls they homeschooled or sang with and taught verses to and who "should know better"—are now living with their boyfriends or their lesbian girlfriends, and these women are wondering why God isn't holding up His part of the bargain.

And I've shared coffee and tears with dear friends who admit that they never feel as if they measure up and they hope someone can magically make them better.

Why did I write this book? Because I love women and I love Jesus, and like a good friend of both, I want to introduce them to each other. Maybe they've met before, but I'm sure that if they spend time together, everything will change.

The Facebook Post That Sparked It All

In the early fall of 2013, I posted the following on my Facebook page:

> Okay, friends . . . I need your help. I'd like to know the dumbest things people tell women they have to do in order to be godly. Ready . . . *Go*!

I thought I might get a few responses, but what happened over the next twenty-four hours was mind boggling—and frankly pretty troubling. Nearly twenty thousand women read the post, and almost five hundred responded. And that was all within twenty-four hours! I knew that women felt burdened and wearied by to-do lists, suggested steps for improvement, and bad advice, but I didn't have any idea how much frustration, anger, angst, and despair was simmering just beneath the surface of so many hearts.

I already knew that women were worn down, because I've had the opportunity to speak with hundreds of them as I've traveled around the country speaking at churches and women's conferences over the past decade or so. And I want to be really clear about something here: my experience with burdened women has not been primarily with those who haven't yet come to faith. No, it is with women who self-identify as Christians, who regularly attend church, who agree that Jesus is the truth and that the truth is supposed to set them free.

And the churches where I met these women aren't what one might call the First Church of Feel-Good-Now. No, these are churches where the Word of God is taught and where women are encouraged to take the call to discipleship seriously. These are serious women—women who would say that their faith in Christ is the most important thing about them. And yet there they were, telling me through tears that they were drowning in to-do lists and dying for some good news.

Based on feedback I've gotten from women I've met face-to-face at conferences, from those who replied to my question on Facebook, and from those who were part of focus groups, I know there is an undeniable groaning among women in what we might call modern American evangelicalism. I felt it myself as I struggled for years trying to be a great mom, a good wife, and a faithful friend, while spending hours at the gym and insisting that everyone else live a life that met what I thought were God's expectations. I carried a burden of responsibility for everyone else's success . . . all the while knowing I was failing. Yet even I was surprised at the depth of anger and despair my question evoked. The responses confirmed something I've long suspected: the landscape that evangelical women live in is a howling wilderness littered with the blood, sweat, and tears of thousands of hardworking, weary women . . . and also with the carcasses of the faith some of them have shed as they've given up in despair and exhaustion.

We've missed the point. We've majored on the minors and

Bad Advice WOMEN RECEIVE

What are the dumbest things people tell women they have to do in order to be godly?

(These are real responses to the question I posted on Facebook.)

- Decorate your home like a magazine.
- Cook only healthy, organic food for the family.
- Don't work outside the home for money.
- Don't be a leader, and don't come up with ideas for ministry. If you do come up with ideas, pretend like they came from your husband.
- Always submit.
- Have a daily Proverbs 31 checklist.
- Have an organized, clean, and "Pinterest-inspired" home. If Jesus were to knock on your door, you'd want Him to be pleased with what He saw.
- Women can "share" or give a greeting in church, but this should not be done from the pulpit—only

failed to fill the hearts of women with the only news that will set them free.

The Source of the Bad News

So where on earth are women getting all this heart-crushing, joy-stripping, bad advice? Everywhere we look. Yes, we get it in church, but we also get it in the checkout line at the grocery store. All we have to do is look up from our groceries off the platform and behind a portable podium or music stand.

- Be the perfect housekeeper, wife, and mother. All the time.
- Master the arts of cooking, sewing, home decorating, gardening, canning, knitting, crocheting, and making the perfect piecrust.
- Be at your husband's sexual beck and call—and like it.
- Make sure your children always obey.
- Participate in every church activity. Do, do, do—all the time!

THE *Good News*

We know that a person is not justified by works of the law but through faith in Jesus Christ, so we also have believed in Christ Jesus, in order to be justified by faith in Christ and not by works of the law, because by works of the law no one will be justified. GALATIANS 2:16

while fumbling for our ATM card, and we see headlines that function as hope-crushing rules:

- Zumba Your Way to Buns of Steel!
- Learn the Mystical Secrets to Great Sex So He'll Never Wander!
- 36 Recipes for Tummy-Satisfying Foods on a Pauper's Budget!

- Save the Planet (or the Whales or the Polar Ice Caps or Unwanted Puppies or . . .)!
- Seven Ways to Guarantee a Promotion!

The bad news creeps in when we're pressured to join this celebrity's nonprofit or sign that petition on the way out of the store . . . assuming, of course, that we donated to whatever charity was selling chocolate bars on the way in (which, by the way, we must never eat!) so that we can have a cause and feel virtuous as we heft our groceries into the back of our environmentally sensitive minivan, which leaves only a teeny-tiny carbon footprint on the planet.

We watch the local news and get reprimanded by the news anchor (aka the News Nanny) for giving our children sugar, caffeine, or fat, or for letting them play video games more than thirty-two minutes per day.

We read fiction books that portray women as weaklings whose theological insights were picked up in two summers of learning how to be like Esther or Ruth at vacation Bible school and who are unable to go through life without Mr. Right (who just happens to be Amish). Or, even more sadly, we read "romance" novels that tell us our womanhood is to be defined by our sexuality and our ability to achieve orgasm the first time, every time, with Mr. Right.

When we read "Christian" nonfiction books, we tend to read titles that are nothing more than the to-do lists, steps, and bad advice *du jour* pumped out by the world, baptized by a few out-of-context Bible verses. We're told that our children must behave in church, have coordinating outfits, and close their eyes when they pray, and that we are responsible for building their self-esteem, even (or perhaps especially) when they fail. We are warned that our children's spiritual well-being (along with their physical and emotional well-being) depends on our ability to feed them home-cooked organic meals, sew all their clothing, have a Pottery Barn–worthy living room, make Pinterest-inspired crafts for every holiday, and post cute pictures of our happy family online. We're to live strictly on a budget, shun a career, never disagree with our husbands, never raise our voices in frustration, and religiously slather our children with SPF 70 PABA-free sunscreen and put UV-protective eye gear on them before they venture out of the house, even if we live in Anchorage and it's January. In a word, we're exhausted.

We're told that our husband's ability to lead depends on our ability to create a spiritual vacuum in the relationship that we hope will eventually suck him into his role as the head of the home. If we fail to submit properly, he'll never experience the respect and the wild, testosterone-fueled freedom that his masculinity requires. We have to be the Proverbs 31 woman 24-7-365, or all will be lost. In other words, our husband's success as a godly man is entirely dependent on our success at being a "godly" woman—as if success were a Christian construct or as if our sanctification depended on anyone other than Christ.

And that's to say nothing about one of the major sources of guilt, shame, and law in a woman's life: her body. It's not just that we shouldn't look like a middle-aged, slightly pudgy woman trying to hide her muffin top beneath three layers of SPANX. We're supposed to look like a Nike triathlete supermodel who has had breast augmentation and spends six hours every day working out, even though she gave birth to five children, nursed them all until her breasts rested on her knees, and stayed up all night rocking the littlest, who just wouldn't stop crying.

And, of course, there's the goddess of exercise, to whom we must offer up vials of sweat every day or we feel so guilty we snap at our families and forget our identities as daughters of the King and instead feel like Jabba the Hutt. We're filled with guilt, exhausted, and terrified that Triathlete Woman will make a move on our stifled, wild-at-heart man.

We're told it is our responsibility to make sure the house is bacteria and virus exempt, the rescue dog eats gluten-free food, and the children are well mannered, cleaned, brushed, ironed, vaccinated (or not, depending on one's views on naturopathic medicine), and properly shorn. We need to make sure our husbands are completely satisfied on every level, the church is well staffed, the neighborhood is evangelized, and the world is prayed for. In other words, we've been told and we believe (at least in part) that the success of everything within our sphere of influence rests on our shoulders and that we'd better get it together before it's too late.

And we're weary.

This kind of exhaustion reminds me of the scene from the 1982 Steven Spielberg movie *Poltergeist*, in which the mom, played by JoBeth Williams, is drowning in an unfinished pool filled with rainwater, mud, and skeletons.[1] The more she struggles to get out of the pool, the more it caves in on her and the more her terror grows.

I know that women (and men) have been overwhelmed by to-do lists, steps, and bad advice since the beginning of time. Even five hundred years ago, Martin Luther didn't need to read his Facebook friends' posts about their having fun without him to realize that there was something wanting in his life. He was aware of his inability to obey God's law from the heart, and he knew he didn't have his own self-approval, let alone God's. But I do think there is something a little more desperate, more frenetic about our present wilderness. There are so many messages being broadcast at us from every direction about "How to be perfect in 149 simple steps" or "How your life will become a self-inflicted Armageddon if you don't follow these rules."

As a woman who loves Christ, the gospel, her family, her church, and her country, I'm standing up to scream, "Stop this madness! Be done with the fluff, the bricks, and the despair-breeding, anxiety-multiplying self-righteousness! It's time to trust in Christ—and Christ alone! He has already done it all. Everything you need has already been given to you." Or in the words of the writer to the Hebrews, "Whoever has entered God's rest has also rested from his works as God did from his. Let us therefore strive to enter that rest" (Hebrews 4:10-11).

My sisters, the Bible has surprisingly good news for you. You can rejoice and rest in all that Jesus has done. My hope is that by the end of this book, you are able to breathe a great big sigh of relief and say, "Whew. He really does love me, and that's all that matters." Yes, He really will make good on His promise: "Come to me, all who labor and are heavy laden, and *I will give you rest*" (Matthew 11:28, emphasis added).

CHAPTER I

HOW DID WE END UP HERE?

So HOW DID WE end up here, with so many to-do lists, so
many steps, and such an overabundance of bad advice? How
is it that women feel so exhausted and are filled with so much
despair? How did many of us fall into the belief that everything depends on us and that we've got to get it right or
everything will go wrong?

As a woman who has attended church nearly every Sunday
since the summer of 1971, when I was first brought to faith
at the age of twenty, I think that much of this bad news
comes from the Christian community and the church itself.
I say this with trepidation and great sadness, so please let me
explain. But first, let me make this clear: the church has not
been the only source of bad advice I've received. Much of the
bad news has come from the world, and much of it is simply

from my own heart. We'll talk more about that later, so for now let's return to how the church has shaped and added to the burden that is crushing women and making us weary.

I've heard countless messages about how I need to do better and try harder and never be satisfied until "my good is better and my better is best." I admit that it has been hard for me to be hopeful that I could ever make the grade as a "godly" woman and live my life in a way that would bless others and bring glory to God. No, let me rephrase that. It's been *impossible* for me to hope I could do everything and be all that I was told I should be by all the women (and men) who have brought the law to me without also assuaging my soul's fears with the gospel.

I've Got a Couple of Free Minutes . . .

That's not to say I didn't try to follow all the rules of Christian womanhood. I recall one afternoon about thirty years ago when it occurred to me that my hope to meet everyone's expectations was driving me (and everyone around me) a bit nuts. Aside from caring for our young family, composed of my husband and me, our three young kids, a dog, and some rowdy chickens, I also taught full-time in the Christian school associated with our church, was a deaconess, sang in the choir, went to church at least three times a week (more if there was a "revival" going on), and generally worked myself into an exhaustion-induced coma every day. To say that I was irritable and weary would be an understatement.

On that particular afternoon, when I realized that I actually had a few hours to spare, I decided to make a new vest for our daughter Jessica's school uniform. In the midst of my harried pinning and cutting of the pattern, I looked at my husband, Phil, and joked, "I must have some guilt I'm trying to work off." We both laughed and shook our heads, but I was more right about that than I knew at the time. Because although I was a Christian and believed that Jesus had died for my sins, I didn't understand what that meant about my guilt. I didn't know that I was justified—or even what justification meant. And so I worked and worked and slaved away for decades, trying to prove that I wasn't the lazy, degenerate loser I used to be (and secretly feared I still was). I was never very happy, and all the people around me knew it. My unhappiness frequently demonstrated itself in self-indulgence (usually overeating) and in anger at anyone else who wasn't working as hard as I was.

I don't completely blame the church I was a part of in those days for my ignorance of the good news, although the truth is, I don't remember ever hearing it. What I heard consisted instead of a steady stream of messages about how I needed to do more and try harder and get really serious about working in and for the church. I needed to get rid of the sin in my life so I could be a victorious Christian and "go in and possess the land" (whatever that meant).

But my problem wasn't only with what I heard (or didn't hear) in church. It was also with messages that I heard in the broader Christian community. I was reading a lot of books about how to be a "godly" woman, but these messages only multiplied my guilt and splintered my soul. I knew I was really messed up and needed to learn how to be a better wife and mother, and this litany of rules seemed to be the very thing I needed. But it was like the Turkish delight the White Witch gave Edmund in *The Lion, the Witch and the Wardrobe*: it tasted really good at first, but it never satisfied my hunger and always left me aching for more.

Instead of freeing me to love and serve Christ and my family, all this "good advice" loaded me down with guilt and shame over my ongoing sin and piled on more and more wearisome rules. The very thing I was taking as an antidote for my failure was making me more and more ill. Instead of finding freedom, I was a slave to self-justification. And judging from what I've heard from other women, I don't think I'm the only one who has ingested this poisonous brew.

Feminism: The Good, the Bad, and the Ugly

Beginning in the nineteenth century in the United States, women sought to obtain equal rights with men in a number of areas, including the home, the workplace, the church, and the halls of government. In the 1800s, coverture laws were passed that finally allowed women to own their own property, even if they were married. It's hard to believe now, but there was a time when a woman couldn't inherit property or claim ownership, and without a husband, she would have to be dependent on her father or another male relative, or she'd become destitute. In 1919 the Nineteenth Amendment to the Constitution at last granted women the right to vote in the United States.

The quest for equal rights didn't end with the right to vote; women have been fighting for equal rights under the law ever since. Much of this effort has resulted in great good, such as giving women the right to hold public office, enter into legal agreements, get an education, and receive equal pay for equal work. Some of the results, such as on-demand abortion, have resulted in deep and heartbreaking evil.

In the 1970s, as the sometimes misguided cry for equality grew, the church began to respond to what it viewed as the threat of feminism. The evangelical church focused its response in three key areas: defining men's and women's roles in the home and the church, taking a stand against abortion (which was legalized in 1973), and opposing the Equal Rights Amendment. But it wasn't until 1979, with the release of Francis Schaeffer's and C. Everett Koop's groundbreaking book and film series *Whatever Happened to the Human Race?* that the evangelical church began to awaken and respond to the horrors of abortion and then, by extension, to the feminist movement in America.[2]

At the same time, with the ordination of women in more liberal denominations, people started to ask questions about equality for women in formerly male-dominated leadership roles in the church. So churches began to formulate answers, set guidelines, produce literature, and host conferences to define and explain gender roles. Hence, the "biblical masculinity" and "biblical femininity" movements were born in the 1980s, reaching their full saturation in the evangelical church's culture by the early 2000s.

Generally speaking, biblical masculinity and femininity may be defined as the recognition that both men and women are equally created in the image of God but also have distinct masculine and feminine roles as part of God's created

Bad Advice WOMEN RECEIVE

What are the dumbest things people tell women they have to do in order to be godly?

(These are real responses to the question I posted on Facebook.)

- Refrain from reading the Bible or praying with your children so you don't usurp your husband's leadership.
- To have a "quiet and gentle spirit," you literally have to be quiet and gentle.
- Must be a stay-at-home mom.
- Be Mary *and* Martha.
- Get married and have children.
- Have *lots* of children.
- Look like June Cleaver by six o'clock in the morning.
- Study how to clean your house and cook.
- Don't be too smart so you won't intimidate men.

order. Those roles are expressed beautifully in the relationship between Christ and His bride, the church.[3]

Much of the material produced by the biblical masculinity and femininity movement has brought great good to many people. For one thing, it has emphasized the importance of marriage and commitment to family. Thanks in part to "no fault" divorce (beginning in 1969 in California and spreading to nearly every state in the union by 1983), the American culture began to experience the breakdown of the traditional

- If you are in the right place with God, you will meet your husband-to-be.
- Be a Proverbs 31 woman: tend to your husband and children, tend to the home, make your husband look good, be good with arts and crafts, make money to add to the family income, and look beautiful all the time.
- Be perfectly feminine.
- Don't be ambitious.
- Read the most current Christian book about how to be a godly wife.
- Consider marriage and motherhood your highest callings.

THE *Good News*

Christ is the end of the law for righteousness to everyone who believes. ROMANS 10:4

home. At least half of an entire generation of children were being raised in single-parent homes where traditional gender roles were not modeled. In addition, many children (including myself) were raising themselves while their parents (or parent) worked.

To say that I personally had no clue what it meant to be defined as a woman according to a biblical understanding would be an understatement. I had never seen how a loving servant leader would care for and provide for his family. I had never seen my mother model joyous support of her husband. What I did see was my mother working at least one full-time job and trying with all her might to provide for my brother and me. I never knew what it meant to be in a family, to work together for a common goal, to live intentionally as the person I had been created to be. Because of that, when I married, I had a lot of learning to do.

Let me say it again: I am very thankful for many of the values and much of the material produced by the leaders of this movement. I am also grateful for the courageous stand that they have taken against strong anti-God, antifamily forces in our culture, for their love for women and men and families, and for their love of the Word and the church.

But as with any movement that gains an audience and influence, the gender roles movement has also produced unfortunate misunderstandings and excesses. Due to a mis-interpretation of biblical teachings, some materials have been produced that do not serve women well. To-do lists, steps, and bad advice have burgeoned, and many women find them-selves exhausted and crushed by the dos and don'ts given to them in the name of biblical womanhood. Essentially we're told that we need to do more, be more, and perform more to be acceptable in God's eyes.

If you're wondering what form some of these steps, lists, and bad advice can take, you can glance through the side-bars throughout this book. These are just a few samples of the hundreds of responses given to me by women who have been harmed by this misunderstanding of what the Bible says about men and women.

The truth is that both radical feminism—lies sold to women in the name of equality—and radical femininity—lies sold to women in the name of Christianity—have harmed women and children. But while Christians have been quick to engage in conversations about the repercussions of misguided feminism, there hasn't been much acknowledgment of the way women are harmed when they are force-fed rules that go beyond Scripture and add to Scripture—rules that are products of a particular culture rather than of the gospel.

For instance, some people have taken the command in Ephesians 5:33 that a wife should respect her husband to mean that a man's masculinity and leadership depend solely on his wife's ability to be feminine. Some have misinterpreted Titus 2:4-5 to mean that a child's godliness and success depend entirely on his or her mother and her daily goodness, consistency, and healthy meal planning. And based on a misunderstanding of 1 Timothy 5:9-14, single women have been told that they have no value apart from a relationship to a man. This is simply ridiculous.[4]

The Proverbs 31 Woman

In an effort to formulate a biblical response to the gender-blurring roles developed by feminism, Christians did what they ought to do: they went to the Bible to see what roles the Bible lays out for women. In that search, they held up several passages as models for determining a woman's role, foremost among them Proverbs 31, Ephesians 5, Titus 2, and 1 Peter 3.

This wasn't a bad place to start, but the principles were often taken out of the larger context of Scripture.

Dr. Jerram Barrs, a professor and Francis Schaeffer scholar, says that this overly narrow focus about women's roles has caused significant damage, leading the Christian community to see women *"entirely through the eyes of men reacting to feminist emphases* by focusing all their deliberation on those four passages."[5] He continues, "I am not saying that those passages should be ignored or set aside, for they are, of course important, but beginning and ending with them has given rise to *severe misconceptions.*"[6]

Do you think that perhaps I'm overstating the problem here? I assure you that I am not. The Proverbs 31 woman has been written about in more than twenty books in just the last decade, ranging from workbooks to how-tos to steps in becoming a woman of virtue in thirty-one days (calendars included). And nearly ten books about becoming a Titus 2 woman have been written in the last decade.[7]

Many women look at these descriptions of the ideal woman and think, *There's no way I could pull that off—no way I could fit that mold.* I don't blame them. Other women work their fingers to the bone in the hope that on some future date their children will rise up and call them blessed. The number of sermons preached on Proverbs 31 and Titus 2 on Mother's Day is enough to tempt women to stay home, not wanting to hear again the ways they're failing.

Of course, the church isn't the only place women are receiving a flood of to-do lists, steps, and bad advice. But because the church's message carries more weight with

Christian women than other sources do, it is particularly destructive. Christian women want to please the Lord; we want to live in a way that positively impacts our children. We are, for the most part, serious about wanting to shine in our part of the dark world, so when the church speaks, we listen.

The problem comes when women (and men) haven't learned how to differentiate between law and gospel—when we don't understand how the good news of Jesus' perfect life, death, resurrection, ascension, and reign is meant to impact us. When we don't see the connection between the righteous life Jesus lived and our standing before a holy God, we are setting ourselves up for bondage. Many women don't understand the freedom that has been purchased for us, and we often get tangled up in legalism or moralism. We don't know what it would look like for obedience to be motivated by gratitude.

A Ministry of Death

Paul described the law as "the ministry of death, carved in letters on stone," which "came with such glory that the Israelites could not gaze at Moses' face because of its glory" (2 Corinthians 3:7). Even the law in its purest form can only accomplish what the law by itself will always accomplish: it will always produce death.

My friends, if even God's law, written directly by His own finger and full of so much glory that it transfigured Moses' face, is a "ministry of death" to those who try to fulfill it, then these to-do lists, steps, and pieces of ludicrous advice will not produce the fruit we're hoping for. They will not build or protect the family or God's people in the world. They will not glorify Him. They will not make Him smile. They will only breed pride, despair, exhaustion, anger, self-pity, hypocrisy, addiction to introspection, and even abandonment of the faith.

I believe there are specific instructions in Scripture regarding gender roles, including those in Genesis 2–3, Proverbs 31, Ephesians 5, 1 Timothy 2, Titus 2, and 1 Peter 3. I believe that these truths remain valid for today and that we ignore them to our great harm. But I also believe that much of what has been dished out to women under the guise of "biblical gender roles" has failed us in at least two ways. It has gone way beyond Scripture's bounds, while at the same time closing off much of the Bible's message of comfort and hope. In these ways, much of this teaching resembles Jesus' description of the Pharisees', for it gathers unnecessarily heavy burdens and lays them on women's shoulders (see Matthew 23:4). Meanwhile, those who teach these things effectively "shut the kingdom of heaven in [their] faces" (verse 13).

When we define gender roles too narrowly, overemphasizing a limited number of texts while completely ignoring the breadth of Scripture—when we try to make Scripture say more than it actually does or tell any segment of people that only certain parts of the Scripture concern them (whether we intentionally communicate this message or not)—we do so to the detriment of women and men, and to the detriment of the church and its mission in the world.

Here are just a few of the unnecessary burdens women are often made to bear. Single women are made to feel that

I feel a lot of pressure to be a "godly" wife and a "godly" mom—and that there's a very narrow definition of what that looks like. The list of things I need to do to fulfill those callings is really long (and impossible): have a perfectly decorated and immaculate home, make all my own food from scratch, feed my family three perfectly balanced meals with ideal nutrition, study the Bible every day, pray often, never yell at my children, provide my kids with enriching educational opportunities every day, be frugal and under budget every month, exercise frequently, have immaculate personal grooming, be a fun mom who is also excellent at godly discipline and instructing, pursue my children's hearts, pursue romance and physical intimacy with my husband, disciple other women in the church, be completely content and fulfilled at home but also find something really valuable to do in my community and church to serve others, host others in my home—the list just keeps on going! I've heard that in order to be the woman God wants me to be, I need to suffocate my feisty personality and be quiet and demure. But I believe God is bigger than these small boxes of what a woman should look like. After all, He's the One who gave me this personality in the first place!

One Woman's
STORY

they are "less than" other women; women who are gifted for a career are made to feel that college or a career is a waste of time and that these women are resisting "God's best" for them. Women whose interests, giftings, and opportunities do not fit the mold of post-industrial-revolution suburbia are disdained by other women who have been gifted with husbands, fruitful uteruses, and inclinations that better portray what has been elevated to the greatest expression of godliness for a woman: the stay-at-home mom. And stay-at-home moms are weighted with additional pressures: it's not enough to be home; they must also serve on every committee, live in a perfectly decorated (and always clean) house, and have perfectly behaved children.[8]

Jesus and the Women He Loved

It's interesting to note that nowhere in Scripture does Jesus fuss with women about embracing what we might consider feminine roles; in fact, He chided Martha for assuming that Mary's theological studies and worship at His feet were less necessary than hospitality and making sandwiches (see Luke 10:41-42). Jesus never chastised the many women who left their homes and followed Him around, providing for His physical needs.

> The twelve were with him, and also some women
> who had been healed of evil spirits and infirmities:
> Mary, called Magdalene, from whom seven demons
> had gone out, and Joanna, the wife of Chuza,

Herod's household manager, and Susanna, and many
others, who provided for them out of their means.
LUKE 8:1-3

Notice that Jesus didn't tell Mary Magdalene to go find
a husband, settle down, and have a family, nor did He tell
Joanna that her place was at home with Chuza, grinding
wheat for wholesome sandwiches. He invited women to step
outside their culturally defined roles and follow Him, and He
allowed them to support Him out of their means.

Paul and the Women He Loved

Paul spent time living in the household of a successful
businesswoman named Lydia, who was his first convert from
Philippi (see Acts 16:11-14). He also had obvious respect
for the deacon-patroness Phoebe, a woman who delivered
one of the most important letters ever written—the one Paul
wrote to the church in Rome.[9] Then there was Priscilla the
tentmaker, who along with her husband corrected Apollos's
doctrine (see Acts 18:26). Scripture doesn't indicate that Paul
had any conversations with any of these women about how
they really ought to be home tidying up and having more
children, or if they were single, how they should be making
themselves available to single guys. Surely if Lydia, Phoebe,
or Priscilla were out of line by stepping outside the kitchen
and the bedroom, someone would have said something about
it, and we'd have a record of it today.

Yes, there are passages in Scripture—especially in Paul's
epistles—about women's roles. But it is biblically untenable

and soul crushing to tell a woman that the only worthwhile activity she can do is to birth children and serve a husband and a family. This mind-set also creates an idol out of the family structure, making success as a homemaker/mother the most important vocation in a woman's life. And although this is a high calling, it should not trump our first and foremost calling: to believe in Christ.

In response to the evils of radical feminism, which shamed women who didn't work outside the home, the radical femininity movement has shamed Christian women who work outside the home (for a variety of reasons) or who are not married or who have been divorced. Many Christian women have been taught that motherhood is not only their highest calling but also that it is the *only* calling they should aspire to. It seems a little like the drunk man who falls off his horse on one side and climbs back into the saddle, only to fall off on the other.

Your Highest Calling

Motherhood is not a woman's only calling, nor is it her highest calling, just as fatherhood is not a man's highest or only calling. The Bible never makes such a claim, and shaming women who want to work in the marketplace (or have to) is unkind, unwise, and unbiblical. While it should be obvious that the Proverbs 31 woman does not fit the mold of a 1950s suburban housewife, that poor horse has been flogged to death by people telling women that the virtuous woman always gets up early and makes organic oatmeal for her family because the spiritual, emotional, and physical well-being of everyone within her sphere of influence depends on her fulfilling her motherly role and being sure that her kids are regular.

Please don't misinterpret what I am saying. If a woman is blessed to have a husband who is able to financially support the family, and if she is gifted with children, I do believe that the best thing she can do is to be home with them. But many women simply do not have the option of staying home, even if they dearly want to. And perhaps more significantly, that is not a woman's highest calling, nor is it the only work her Savior has called her to.

I believe in the infallibility and timelessness of Scripture, and I would never want to discard the Bible's instructions about women and the way we've been designed. At the same time, though, many churches have blindly embraced twenty-first-century, post-industrial-revolution suburbia, where Hubby leaves the home to go to work during the day while the wife stays home with the kiddies, as the sole option for a woman who wants to be godly. We've bought into the notion that a woman who loves God should look like June Cleaver, the 1950s paragon of virtue, with her pearls and her crisply ironed dresses. These lockstep demands do not allow for differences in life circumstances, temperament, or gifting. Meanwhile, talented Christian women are being thwarted, crushed, disrespected, and manhandled. And many of them are simply giving up in despair, because it is just too painful to try to fit into Cinderella's size-5 glass slipper when you're a size-9 wide (and you prefer flip-flops or tennis shoes).

So if a woman's highest calling isn't to be June Cleaver,

what is it? Jesus addresses our highest calling as women (and men) in John 6, right after He multiplied bread for five thousand hungry wanderers. "What must we do, to be doing the works of God?" they asked (John 6:28). Rather than tell them to get home and get to work, He answered in the most astounding way: "This is the work of God, that you believe in him whom he has sent" (verse 29).

Wait . . . just believe? But what about the work I'm supposed to be doing?

These people wanted to know how to acquire the life-giving bread that Jesus had spoken of. Here was His response: "Do not work for the food that perishes," he told them, "but for the food that endures to eternal life, which the Son of Man will give to you" (John 6:27).

The people wanted to know how to multiply bread, how to do miracles, how to make sure they were earning brownie points and fulfilling their callings. He told them flat out what their calling was: "Believe in Me."

One commentary puts it this way:

> The only "work" that guarantees the possession of this redemptive manna is to believe in Jesus (John 6:29). The gospel sabotages any notion of legalism or performance-based acceptability with God. The only thing we bring to Jesus is our need. All we offer is the admission that we have nothing to offer.[10]

What is our highest calling as women? Our highest calling is to believe. It consists of believing, resting, and rejoicing in the work that has been done for us by the Savior, who perfectly fulfilled every gender role in our place. It might sound strange to think of Jesus fulfilling female gender roles, but He did so by wholeheartedly submitting to His Father's will and making it His own. When He was in the garden of Gethsemane, He gave up His desire to be released from the cup of suffering and placed Himself in submission to His Father's love. Jesus then died for all our skewed ideas about what we must do, all our failure in doing so, and our flat-out rebellion against the added-on laws that have been foisted on us.

Our highest calling is to believe in and love the gospel and then to live our lives in the light of all Jesus has already done for us.

Unbearable Responsibilities

When we try to make the Bible say more than it does by giving secondary passages ultimate authority, or when we snip passages out of context, we end up with nothing more than steps, lists, and bad advice that put women in bondage. Ultimately this leads to either pride (if we feel that we're doing pretty well at our to-do list—or at least better than the people around us) or despair (if we fear we'll never be able to measure up). For most women, the takeaway from all this bad advice has not been the righteousness, peace, and joy we're promised (see Romans 14:17). The takeaway has been unbearable responsibilities.

These misguided teachings burden women by telling us that God is pleased with us based on something other than our faith in Christ and His righteousness. This mind-set crushes women by assigning to us a task we can never fulfill. A wife cannot control her husband's godliness. A mother cannot control her child's faith. A single woman cannot control God's plan for her life. No person can do what only Christ can do. These teachings cause women to try to pressure and manipulate those around us to conform in the hope that when we finally lay our weary heads on our pillows, we can breathe out an exhausted, "What a good girl am I," as we pass into desperately needed sleep. I know this is reality because I lived this lie for decades.

As a young mom, I would get up early in the morning, try to do my daily readings in an attempt to get through the Bible every year, and spend time going over my prayer list. Then I'd get my kids up and ready for school, spend the day teaching, come home, make sure everyone was doing all the things they needed to do, make dinner, clean the kitchen, read godly books to the kids, pray with them, try to create lesson plans, make sure all the animals were fed, try to find good recipes, try to connect with my mom, try to encourage my husband, and then collapse into bed . . . only to do it all over again the next morning. The truth is that I never felt as if I was doing enough, and every time someone in my household failed in any way, I assumed that it was a direct reflection of my own personal failures to do and to be enough.

How Can We Recognize the Good News?

Let me suggest one way for you to begin to judge whether a word you've just heard or read is rooted in grace and flowing from the gospel. If you walk away from church or any other message saying, "I'm going to try really, really, really hard to do better—to be a better woman, wife, mother, daughter, or friend," then you haven't heard the message of the gospel. If you walk away feeling proud of yourself because you've got all those steps covered, then you haven't heard the message of the gospel. If you walk away feeling shamed and full of despair because you know what a loser you are, then you haven't heard the message of the gospel. If you walk away trying to figure out how to get everyone in your family on the same page so you can be successful, then you haven't heard the message of the gospel. You haven't heard the good news. And the good news is the only message that will free you to be the woman Christ has meant for you to be. The good news is what you need to believe. And belief in the good news is the only way for you to find freedom in your identity in Christ.

Questions FOR REFLECTION AND DISCUSSION

1. What to-do lists, steps, or bad advice have people given you as a way to make God happy with you? What impact has this bad news had on your life and your faith?

2. What have you been taught about feminism? What good has come to our society as a result of the quest for equal rights? What harmful side effects have resulted?

3. What have you been taught about "biblical femininity"? What has been helpful for you? What has been harmful?

4. How do you think God sees you and feels about you? What is this impression based on?

5. As you seek to be a godly woman, how often do you remember the gospel?

6. As you look at the way Jesus and Paul interacted with and spoke about women, what stands out to you? Is there anything that surprises you or anything that differs from teachings you've heard in church?

7. Summarize what you've learned in this chapter in four or five sentences.

CHAPTER 2

WHAT EVER HAPPENED TO THE GOOD NEWS?

CHARITY WAS RAISED in a Christian home that was more about rules than about grace. She was told that God would be pleased with her and bless her if she was submissive and quiet, if she grew her hair long, if she never questioned authority, if she learned to be hospitable, and if she never listened to secular music. She had never heard of God's grace—in fact, the only time she heard the word at all was in reference to her sister, whose name was Grace.

Although Charity was told that Jesus died for her sins, she was also told that it was her responsibility to keep God happy and earn His blessing by being obedient. As a sensitive, introspective girl, she knew that God wasn't fooled by the ways she was failing to obey (inwardly, at least). Her conscience was troubled, and she couldn't shake the assumption that God was disappointed with her. Every day she determined to do better, and on the days she succeeded, she grew picky and irritated with her siblings—and then felt condemned again. On the days she failed, she felt utterly hopeless. But she kept trying, because not trying was unthinkable. She feared God in all the wrong ways.

Then the inconceivable happened. Her father, the man she had been taught to love and respect, left the family. Charity immediately assumed that her father's desertion was a sign that God was punishing her for her disobedience. She tried to repent. She made bargains with God, promising that she would never think another bad thought if He would just bring her father back. Her mother tried to reassure her that her father hadn't left them because of some failure on Charity's part, but it didn't help. She continued to spiral downward into a pit of self-loathing, self-harm, and despair.

The reason Charity wasn't helped by her mother's attempts to reassure her was because Charity had already bought into the soul-crushing lessons of moralism: if you do good things, God is obligated to bless you; if you do bad things, God will punish you. She thought that everything in her life rested on her faithful obedience. So when tragedy struck, she assumed it came from the hand of an angry God who had finally gotten fed up with her failures. Eventually Charity left the home and what she thought was Christianity. She decided that God (if there even was a God) was way too hard to please and that she was way too weak to obey.

Although she was eventually reconciled to her mother,

her heart had been too battered to ever venture out into a life of faith again. It was easier for her to pretend she'd never heard about Jesus than to try to live up to all the demands she thought He'd placed on her.

The truth is that Charity never really heard the true gospel message. She was rejecting an empty shell of moralism . . . and I didn't blame her. Moralism is not good news. "Work hard and God will bless you" is bad news. Women don't need to learn steps to make God happy. They need to hear the good news of the Christian message: God is already pleased with us if we are in His Son.

A pastor recently made this bold claim about Christianity in our culture: "As far as Western civilization is concerned, Christendom is officially dead."[11] Although that might sound like a bit of a stretch in some parts of the country, I believe it. I've traveled all across America in my speaking, and I've witnessed this change of landscape firsthand. Whether or not you're feeling the effects of it yet, the society we live in is now utterly secular and markedly anti-Christian . . . and the future of the church's liberties here does not look bright.

By agreeing with the claim that Christendom is officially dead, I do not mean that the church itself is dead. The church around the world, and the hundreds of thousands of expressions of the church, even in our secularized nation, are not dead. There are millions of true believers and many faithful pastors all across this country, and I am thankful for them.

The church itself will persevere in whatever culture it finds itself for one reason: the church's Husband, the Lord of the church, will surely sustain His bride. We may suffer martyrdom, but the church will be victorious—of that I have no doubt. Secularism will not be able to stamp out the voice of the church any more than emperor worship, paganism, the Enlightenment, socialism, communism, or materialism could. Jesus will have His bride. No other religion or secular humanism will ultimately prevail. Jesus didn't die to bring a wife to Himself only to have her slain by those who despise Him. I've read the end of the story: Jesus wins. Yes, our country may be headed for a new dark age, but this nation and the church are not analogous. America may fall, but the church will stand triumphant forever (see Matthew 16:18).

So when I agree that Christendom in the United States is dead, this is what I mean: our culture is no longer one that understands even the most basic principles of Christianity. The good news of the work of Jesus Christ (or even the most basic principles of the Christian religion) is simply not familiar to many Americans. In the movie *Gravity*, as the character played by Sandra Bullock faces what she thinks is imminent death, she whispers, "I've never prayed in my life. Nobody ever taught me how."[12] Although this is a fictional example, it makes an interesting statement about our culture's perspective on prayer. Even if people want to pray, many of them have little experience and training about how to do so. In contrast, in the 1950s, most people attended church—if not regularly, then at least on Christmas and Easter. And at a minimum, most people knew how to pray (or sing) the "Our Father." Today, however, the culture is increasingly pluralistic and secular.

While it's clear that this country is moving away from its Christian underpinnings, that's not my main concern.

Christians have always been part of an unbelieving world, and in some ways it might be a good thing that the June Cleavers down the block have shed their veneer of religiosity and are saying they're too busy or too spiritual to care about organized religion anymore. At least that may be a bit more honest than their counterparts from a couple of generations ago.

My primary concern is that thousands of women who would self-identify as Christians don't have the faintest idea what the gospel means. They don't realize that the idea of working our way into God's good graces or trying harder in order to obtain blessings from Him is antithetical to the very nature of the good news.

Be Good = Feel Good = Get Goodies

This empty shell of Christianity—the idea that we earn God's favor with good behavior—is what Christian Smith, in his landmark study of youth and religion in America, labeled "moralistic therapeutic deism."[13] In plainer English, he's saying people are being taught that Christianity consists of these three dogmas: *be good* so you can *feel good* and *God will give you goodies*. And while those tenets might seem like a good idea on the surface, they are nothing more than bad news that will enslave, crush, and deaden our souls. "Be good so you can feel good and get goodies" is *not* Christianity.

Why is it that so many of us have swallowed this toxic brew? Why are we missing out on the sweet refreshment of the gospel? How is it that the faith that once turned the world upside down (see Acts 17:6) has been boiled down to

Bad Advice WOMEN RECEIVE

What are the dumbest things people tell women they have to do in order to be godly?

(These are real responses to the question I posted on Facebook.)

- Be at church every time the doors are open. Teach a Bible club, even if you're not gifted at teaching or working with kids.
- Never show anyone your true self. It's not pretty, and we're supposed to be perfect.
- God will give you the desires of your heart if you obey Him.
- Make your own laundry detergent and buy only organic, nonprocessed foods you grow yourself. And, of course, breast-feed.
- If you have any sort of struggle or problem in your life, you shouldn't be seeking to serve anywhere.
- Smile all the time. Keep your problems to yourself. Never let anyone know you are struggling.
- Do everything you are asked to do at church. Never say no to a ministry opportunity.

dreary steps, lists, and bad advice? I'm sure that, at least in part, it's because most of us haven't been taught the basics of our faith. Sadly, many churches have failed to teach the Bible and have instead tried to amuse, cajole, prod, or entertain seekers into the Kingdom. But that's not the only problem.

- Don't rest or nap during the day when you're tired. Stay busy at all times, or you risk giving the devil a foothold through your idleness.
- Don't have an epidural during childbirth—you shouldn't try to escape the Curse.
- Never admit you're struggling, because that means you're simply not obeying the Lord.
- Don't say no to anyone who makes a request of you.
- If someone asks you how you are, even if your world is upside down, smile and say, "Better than I deserve!" Don't be too transparent. People need you to be stable.
- Your husband's happiness is fully your responsibility.
- Since Jesus died for you, if you are thankful and really love Him, you'll always be at church and study the Bible hard core every day. You'll give away all your money and lead every study and save all the people and serve every human being.

THE *Good News*

There is therefore now no condemnation for those who are in Christ Jesus. ROMANS 8:1

Even in churches that would say that they are expositional in their preaching and are concerned with right doctrine, many women's ministries are notorious for their fluffiness and inanity. Women are invited to conferences where they learn to smile a lot because that makes the people around them happier.

They're offered classes in folding napkins that look like empty tombs so that their tables can reflect the Resurrection. Even in serious churches, it is sometimes insinuated—even asserted—that the study of doctrine or theology is only for the guys. Women are told that they should content themselves with learning new recipes, taking care of their bodies, or beautifying their homes, while leaving the weightier matters of doctrine to the men. After all, women are told, they are more easily deceived than men and should therefore avoid any study aside from what they learn from their husbands or their pastors.[14] Any woman who spends too much time studying is probably usurping her husband's role. When women do study the Bible, they're often told that their study of the Bible should be restricted to typical quasi-Christian stereotypes.

Somehow many churches miss the poignant portrait of how Jesus treated one woman who wanted to learn theology. The account of Mary at the feet of Jesus should free every woman to spend as much time as she can with Him and learn all she can about Him, for He told Martha "one thing is necessary" . . . and surprisingly, it isn't fussing with the lunch. Jesus said that learning of Him is the "good portion, which will not be taken away from her" (Luke 10:42).

Moralism: Karma for Christians

Most of us know that Jesus was born in Bethlehem, that He died on the cross, that He rose again, and that we should read our Bibles and pray. But if we dig deeper than that, we find that we're pretty confused about our faith.

Thankfully, however, Jesus doesn't love us because we're good theologians. That's a good thing, because none of us would qualify. We don't love God with our whole minds, as we're commanded to do in Matthew 22:37. No, Jesus loves us because He has simply chosen to do so, not because of anything good in us or because He thinks we're really smart or because we have such good theological potential. No, He loves us simply out of the generosity of His loving heart.

Even so, not knowing about Him and all He has done for us leaves us open to be ensnared in all sorts of error and bondage. We've fallen prey to the moralism that defines every godless culture, and we are now firm believers in karma—the idea that if you act right, you'll feel good and good things will happen to you.

Whenever a society, church, movement, family, or individual loses sight of the centrality of the gospel of grace, a different religion will always fill the void. Something will hold the gravitational center; there will always be a polestar around which we will orbit. And when it isn't the good news of the work of Jesus, it will inevitably be a religion of bad news—a religion of works and merit, a religion of "what goes around comes around." In other words, it will always degenerate into karma. Every other religion in the world is based on the principle of karma: *be good* so you can *feel good* and *good things will happen to you.* This is not Christianity. Christianity stands in direct opposition to works-based religion and karma.

The principle of karma is everywhere—even in nonreligious settings. For instance, karma is the driving principle behind every educational system: work hard so you can get good grades, and then you'll feel good about yourself, land a good job, buy good stuff, have a good family, and eventually retire to southern Florida to gather seashells on the beach while you drink mai tais and feel really good about all you've accomplished.

Karma also drives the self-esteem movement: if you tell children they are good, then they will be good and they'll do good, and good stuff will happen to them. And you'll get to feel good about your parenting. I've even spoken at home-schooling conferences where parents were told that if they feed their children broccoli, they will become little Esthers and Daniels. Here's the karma equation: good veggies in, good kids out (although for the life of me I can't figure out why you'd feed your daughter something that might pre-destine her to life in a pagan king's harem).

Karma is at the heart of the youth sports movement: if children learn a sport, they will feel good about themselves and be part of a group of people who feel good about them-selves. Then they will do good things and good things will happen to them, and they won't do drugs.

Karma is also at the heart of the environmental move-ment: recycle those plastic water bottles (or, better yet, don't even use them), and you'll feel good about yourself, and Mother Nature will be happy with you, and the trees will smile on you. I could go on and on, and I know you could too.

Certainly there are beneficial sides to each of those things I mentioned. Of course it's good for kids to get an education and eat a balanced diet, and I'm in favor of recycling. The

I'll never forget the Christmas Eve service I attended before I met Jesus. I was in my early twenties, attending a church that I now know has good theology and kind members, but what I heard that night was the voice in my own head about how out of place I was in my black dress and ripped nylons. It saddens me now to know that I missed the message of the gospel and Christ's love for me while I worried about my clothes. I think that's still a risk within church culture—the idea that you have to clean yourself up first before you come, whether that means fresh stockings or freedom from habitual sin. The truth is, however, that we can't clean ourselves up on our own. Only Jesus can do that.

One Woman's
—STORY—

trouble comes in when those things start to define us if we do them or guilt-trip us if we don't.

We Just Want to Know We Are Okay

Every one of us is striving to assure ourselves that we are okay. We all long to believe that we're measuring up, being all we should be, and doing the best we can. We want to be able to approve of ourselves, have others approve of us, and most of all, know that God thinks we're okay too. Hundreds of quasi-Christian messages play into this desire by offering to tell us the ten secrets to achieving our full potential or the five habits every mom must master.

We not only want to be okay, but we also want to be free from those suspicions of failure and guilt that gnaw at our souls, those self-accusations that whisper, *Oh, how could you have been such an idiot?* We want to know that we're being good so we can feel good and believe that good things will happen to us. Even if we'd never say we believe in karma, we certainly believe that what goes around comes around. How many times have you said, "He deserved what he got" or "She made her bed; let her lie in it"?

Or perhaps someone has tried to reassure you by saying, "Things look bad right now, but they always work out in the end." Whenever anyone says that to me, I want to say, "How do you know? Do you think they'll work out because I'm a good person? Do good things automatically happen to good people? Since when did karma start trumping Christianity?" But I don't. Usually I just smile and say, "Thanks." (Because I'm a good person and I really want people to like me. Smile intended.)

A few summers ago, I found a cell phone at the beach. I noticed it lying there on the grass, so after several hours, I decided to ask around and see if I could find out who it belonged to. When I talked to one family, the mother replied, "That's so kind of you to care about that. I know good will come to you because you're being so nice." I smiled and said, "Thanks" (for all the reasons mentioned above).

But I'm not always so quiet about my feelings on karma. On another occasion I ran into a woman who had been a friend of my daughter's in high school. She remarked how I was such a wonderful Christian writer and that she knew it was because I was so faithful in serving God. On that occasion, I didn't say thanks. Instead, I made the buzzer noise and said, "No, you're absolutely wrong. God isn't blessing me because I'm good. He's using me because He is good and His Son died in my place." She smiled and wandered off. I suppose she was just expecting me to say thanks. I wonder if she thinks I'm good now.

This desire to be thought of as okay is a central topic at funerals. Typically the minister, family members, and friends of the deceased stand up and talk about what a good person old Joe was. When we do this, we're seeking to justify Joe's existence; we're hoping to say that he really was okay, that his life wasn't a waste of resources, that old Joe really was good old Joe after all, and that we can rest assured that good old Joe is smiling down from heaven on all of us now. We all want to be remembered as people who did good and left the world a better place than it was when we found it. And we think that if we do this, good is bound to come to us and god (whoever that might be for you personally) will smile. Whatever we say with our mouths, our lives prove that we believe in karma.

We Don't Need Karma; We Need Good News

The first problem with this line of thinking is that according to the Bible, none of us is good (see Romans 3:10-12). None of us deserves blessings. We deserve judgment. The thought that we could earn something because of our goodness is patently untrue. Jesus Himself said, "Why do you call me good? No one is good except God alone" (Mark 10:18). God's standard for goodness doesn't merely involve finding the owner of a lost phone. His standard for goodness is perfection: "You therefore must be perfect, as your heavenly Father is perfect" (Matthew 5:48). God defines goodness as having 24-7-365 love for Him and love for our neighbors throughout our lives (see Matthew 22:37-39). We are not good.

The second fallacy with this mind-set is the idea that God is an impersonal force. The Bible doesn't say, "Trust the force, Luke!" The Bible tells us to trust a Person. The belief that there is some sort of impersonal force that causes everything to even out and be fair in the end is not only false but also terrifying. We'd better hope there isn't an impersonal force that is going to pay it forward to us at the end of our lives.

I've done some really terrible stuff (and loads of boringly stupid and selfish stuff), and even after all these years as a follower of Christ, I'm terribly bent toward sin. Karma isn't good news; it's terrifying news, and the only people who think karma is good news are those who are self-assured enough or delusional enough to think they're okay. I don't think I'm okay. I think I'm a great sinner who needs a great Savior. Period. The thought of an impersonal force that will even everything out in the end sends me into a panic.

The real good news is that there is a personal God, not just a force, who has declared that He isn't looking to give us our comeuppance. He sees us as we really are, not as we

ELYSE FITZPATRICK || 37

pretend to be, and yet He loves us so much that He was willing to be separated from His Son and to pour out His wrath on the Son in our place.

Some impersonal force of karma or luck simply does not exist in the universe God has created. Karma, luck, and chance are pagan imaginings—ways to avoid doing business with the living and sovereign Lord of the universe, ways to avoid the humiliation of grace.

Real personal evil in the form of Satan does exist. Real personal good in the form of the triune God also exists. There is a good God. He has made Himself known to us through His Word and through His Son, and He has conquered Satan and defeated sin and death for us. He hasn't given us death, which is the wage our sin has earned. No, He has given us grace instead. Paul described grace this way: "The free gift of God is eternal life in Christ Jesus our Lord" (Romans 6:23).

Grace is the best news any sinner can hear. It is a free gift; it is eternal life for those who deserve death. As Bono, the lead singer of U2, says, "Grace defies reason and logic. Love interrupts, if you like, the consequences of your actions, which in my case is very good news indeed, because I've done a lot of stupid stuff. . . . I'd be in big trouble if Karma was going to finally be my judge. . . . I'm holding out that Jesus took my sins onto the Cross, because I know who I am, and I hope I don't have to depend on my own religiosity."[15]

For some reason we tend to think it's scarier to rely on the grace of a personal God than it is to believe in karma. But grace is not scary! What's really scary is that there might be some loveless, impersonal force that always pays me back

Lies WOMEN ARE TOLD

What false messages have you heard about what God thinks of you?

(The following responses were gathered from focus groups.)

- If you sin, He is disappointed in you because you are failing Him.
- You are such a mess as a wife and mother. How can God ever use you?
- Look at all your friends and how well their lives are going! You will never amount to anything!
- Look how happy everyone else is—God must really be blessing them. And now look at your own life—what a mess! God must hate you!
- People look down on you because of the color of your skin. Even in the church, there is so much discrimination. What makes you think God cares about you?
- God loves whomever He chooses to love. So if you're struggling, there's no guarantee that you're one of the chosen.
- You have been given so much—you are one of the rich people God is talking about. You might be

what I deserve. I would much sooner cast myself on the mercy of a loving God who has demonstrated His goodness by giving me His Son than hope that some imagined mechanism called karma sees the good I do and ignores the bad. I need the good news of the gospel.

condemned because you live in so much comfort compared to the rest of the world.

- You are a failure!
- How do you know you are following God's direction for your life? What if you missed the boat?
- You are failing as a mother. If you can't bring up your children to love Jesus, how will you ever get a "well done" from Him?
- You are wasting your education by staying home with your kids. If you had a paycheck, at least you would be contributing something to society.
- Give up! It's no use trying over and over again. You are bound to fail. God isn't going to help you.
- God wants you to be "good." You're supposed to be a model of perfection, hide your flaws, and work really hard to earn love from people and God.
- Compared to the woman God wants me to be, I'm a disappointment.

THE *Good News*

For freedom Christ has set us free; stand firm therefore, and do not submit again to a yoke of slavery. GALATIANS 5:1

Now, you might be wondering why I'm talking so much about karma in a book about the stupid things women are told about how to please God. But the reason all these steps, lists, and bad advice appeal to us in the first place is because we have bought into the idea of karma.

We think that if we dress in a certain way, we'll be especially blessed and our daughters will be modest and our sons will choose virtuous women to marry. We think that if we birth our children at home, our family will be healthy and unified and our children will bond with us and never leave. We think that if we create a leadership vacuum in our marriage, our husbands will automatically do what they're supposed to do, and we'll be virtuous women, and people will rise up and call us blessed. We think that if we get breast augmentation, our husbands will always love us, or that if we're really modest, their hearts won't be drawn to other women. We think that if we get back to nature (another impersonal force), somehow we'll be blessed with health and life. And we think that the only way God can build His Kingdom is with our dust-free homes.

At the end of the day, at the end of our lives, we want to know we're okay, and we want to know we've achieved success as Christian women. This isn't Christianity. This is karma, and it will either crush our souls or make us proud—or both. I don't know about you, but this way of life scares me to death.

Being Okay Is Not a New Concept

The desire to know we're okay didn't originate with the decline of Christendom in the United States—it has been around much longer than that. In fact, the Bible talks a lot about this longing to feel okay. It just uses a term we don't use much anymore: *justification*.

In the Bible, justification is primarily God focused. We

need to be justified before a holy God, and He is the only One who can provide that.

Justification has two equally important meanings. First, it means complete forgiveness. Sometimes justification is defined as "just as if I had never sinned." That's a great definition, because it captures the idea that the record of all our wrongs has been completely obliterated by Jesus' blood, which was shed for us. Romans 5:18 describes Christ's death on the cross as "one act of righteousness [that] leads to justification and life for all men."

Your okay-ness rests in the fact that God has forgiven all your sins. You don't have to make up for them or try to justify yourself by blaming others or hope that your good outweighs the bad. You are completely forgiven. If you believe, you are no longer under God's judgment for your sin. You are forgiven.

The second meaning of justification refers to complete righteousness. It's not merely a clean record; it is a record of complete obedience. I once heard author Jerry Bridges define it as "just as if I had always obeyed." Jesus Himself has provided the record of complete obedience that we need.

During the years He walked on earth, starting with His birth in Bethlehem, through His childhood in Nazareth, and during His ministry in Israel, Jesus always perfectly fulfilled that command to love 24-7-365. He perfectly loved His Father and His neighbor in our place so that now, when God looks at us, He doesn't see us as lawbreakers or even forgiven lawbreakers. He sees us as *law keepers*.

Isn't that great news? Isn't that so much better than karma?

It's such good news that it's hard to believe. Scripture says that the righteousness of God is available "through faith in Jesus Christ for all who believe" (Romans 3:22).

One of the ways we can get free from the bondage of to-do lists and steps is to remember that we are completely justified. We really are okay right now—and more okay than we ever could have hoped or imagined. We are okay before God, the One who sees us as we really are. We are okay because He has made us completely okay, completely for-given, completely righteous. He has justified us and has done so because He loves us. We don't have to try to justify our-selves anymore. We don't have to try to make Him smile. He is already smiling. There is nothing more we need to make up for or prove or demand. We've been given everything our souls ever needed in Christ—and not because we earned it or because we were really good. It's because *He* is really good. That's really great news, isn't it?

Jesus didn't believe in karma, and His life wasn't a lesson in moralism. What went around from Him didn't come around to Him—at least not during His time on earth. Jesus was the quintessential embodiment of the godly man of Psalm 1, wasn't He? He didn't walk in the counsel of the wicked or stand with sinners or sit with scoffers. His delight was in the law of the Lord, and He meditated on it day and night. But when you look at His life, does it seem that He was "like a tree planted by streams of water" (Psalm 1:3)? Would you say, as you consider the horrors He faced at Golgotha, that "in all that he does, he prospers" (verse 3)? No, He got treated like the wicked—the chaff that is driven away by the wind.

Jesus' righteous life and gruesome suffering should destroy any belief we have in karma. Meanwhile, we've all lived sinful lives, and yet we're treated as though we have obeyed in every way. We, the wicked, are like the well-watered tree, planted by streams of water, "that yields its fruit in its season, and its leaf does not wither" (verse 3).

So what's the takeaway for women in our context? Recycle if you like. But recycling doesn't justify you. Eat organic foods and give birth to eight babies in your bathtub if you like. But whole grains and natural births don't justify you. Walk for whatever cause you like: be pink, be green, or dress in camo print. God isn't impressed. None of those things justifies you.

Homeschool or don't homeschool; be married or don't be married. Live in the city, live on the prairie; love highbrow classical music, groove to Lecrae, or bow humbly before "And Can It Be That I Should Gain?" None of it justifies you; none of it is enough to make you righteous before the Lord. But don't worry—the position of Justifier has been filled. His name is Jesus. You don't need to audition anymore. Rejoice.

The lyrics to Dustin Kensrue's wonderful song "It's Not Enough" speak eloquently of our need for Someone who will be enough on our behalf:

It's not enough, it's not enough
I could walk the world forever
Till my shoes were filled with blood
It's not enough, it's not enough
I could right all wrongs, or ravage
Everything beneath the sun

It's not enough, it's not enough
To make me whole.[16]

Questions FOR REFLECTION AND DISCUSSION

1. The Bible promises blessings for obedience, but these blessings always come as a result of "faith working through love" (Galatians 5:6). Still, even if we have this head knowledge, it's easy to fall into an unintentional belief in karma. Can you see any areas in your life where you've believed that if you did good, good things would automatically happen to you?

2. How would you be able to identify whether you were hoping in a cause to make you okay? For instance, have you ever been angry because you did something good and didn't get "goodies" in return? Have you ever worried that you weren't doing enough good? Can you think of any examples of a belief in karma in your own life?

3. Why would a belief in karma seem like a good thing to unsaved people? Why is it really bad news?

4. What does it mean to be justified? Do you believe that when God looks at you, He sees you as completely righteous? How would believing this change your life?

5. Summarize what you have learned in this chapter in four or five sentences.

CHAPTER 3

LAWS, RULES, STEPS, AND MORE BAD NEWS

WHEN I FIRST BECAME A MOM, I was given some very unhelpful advice from other believers about how to train my children. Much of the advice came from a legalistic (but wildly popular) pamphlet that was going around at the time. It gave instructions for how to break your child's rebellious spirit by forcing him or her to comply with your every desire—even dictating when your baby should eat and sleep. We were told that children should not be allowed to voice their opinions about anything and that instantaneous obedience should be required in every circumstance.

These teachers believed that Paul's prohibition against provoking children to anger (see Ephesians 6:4) was primarily a prohibition against being inconsistent in discipline. I was told that my husband and I represented God to our children and that if they disobeyed us, they would disobey God, too. I actually believed that my children were supposed to think of our authority in the same way they thought of the Lord's. The theory went that if our children disrespected our authority, they would face disastrous consequences later in their lives.

I shudder to think of the number of times I followed this soul-crushing advice and treated my children in a harsh, demanding way. In the midst of this season, it never occurred to me that I had been raised in a completely different environment—a fairly lawless one—and still the Lord had brought salvation to me. While it's true that parents have an important, God-ordained role to play in shaping their children, we need to be wary of any advice that implies that the way a child turns out rests entirely with whether Mom and Dad followed all the parenting rules to a tee.

Sadly, I didn't learn about how to live in the light of God's gracious love until my children were grown and gone. It has been only over the last ten years or so that I've come to understand how the good news of what Jesus has already done should inform my parenting—and now, my grandparenting. Knowing and resting in the truth that Jesus loves sinners has changed the way I respond to my grandchildren when they fail. I find that I have more patience with my kids and my grandkids and that their failures no longer shock or discourage me.

For instance, when my young grandchildren have trouble sharing with one another, I tell them I know what that's like because I have trouble sharing as well. When I get on an airplane, I don't want to share the space next to me. I think I'll be happy if I can have all the room to myself. I admit that I'm just like them—it's just that they fight over toys and I fight over "my" space. Now, rather than shaming my grandchildren by saying things like, "I can't believe you're so selfish not to share your toys!" I can say, "I know what it's like to feel as if I have to have something to be happy. When we know we should share but don't want to, we can go to Jesus, who loves sinners, and ask for His grace."

When Good Advice Goes Bad

Women have been giving and receiving advice ever since there have been sisters, mothers, and daughters. The advice that older women give to younger women about how to live wisely can be a great good. As Paul told Titus, no one is better at training young women than godly older women (see Titus 2). In fact, Proverbs 31 is the record of a mother teaching her son what kind of woman he should look for when he marries. I'm thankful for my mother and my mother-in-law and for all the women who have spoken into my life and helped me become the woman I am today. And I'm thankful that I've had an open door to share wisdom with many women myself—especially my own daughters, and now their daughters too.

But while advice has the potential to help, it also has the potential to harm. Advice becomes unhelpful when it is elevated to the level of inspired Scripture. Likewise, advice is no longer beneficial when women are told that they can earn merit (blessings or goodies) from God by following it. And finally, advice is hurtful when we get our identity from the rules we keep rather than through the work Jesus has accomplished for us. (We will consider the first two of these problems in this chapter, and we'll look at the third in chapter 4.)

Again, let me say that I'm thankful for much of the advice I've been given over the course of my life. Whenever someone tells me about a better way to do something, I'm glad to hear it. However, when I'm told that following a specific piece of advice will make me godlier or will ensure that God will be pleased with me, that advice becomes poisonous to my soul.

Whenever we say that something we do will affect God's disposition toward us, we are elevating it to the level of inspired Scripture. As a result, what might have been a helpful hint will eventually crush us.

Here are some examples to explain what I mean. When God created Eve, He said, "It is not good that the man should be alone; I will make him a helper fit for him" (Genesis 2:18). The New Testament teaches that women are to love their husbands and to be workers at home (see Titus 2:4-5). From these truths, I understand that I am to love and help my husband and that I am to do so, at least in part, by overseeing the work that needs to be done in the home. Okay, so far, so good.

However, these good principles become harmful when I am told that under the title of being a "helper" and a "worker at home" I must iron my husband's shirts immediately upon removing them from the dryer and that doing so will make

God more pleased with me. In this case "prompt shirt iron-ing" becomes a toxic law for me.

Why? Because through my ironing, I am seeking to earn merit or blessings from God. And if I fail to iron, I believe I am liable to judgment. I'm taking what may be a helpful tip and giving it the same weight as inspired Scripture. And along the way I may also be seeking to approve of myself, hoping that even though I yelled at the kids this morning, I'm okay after all. In more medieval terms, I may be seek-ing to earn indulgences for my short temper by my prompt ironing.[17] My ironing becomes penance offered to atone for my sinful anger.

Yes, there are some laws that God has clearly communi-cated to His people. These are unchangeable truths that reflect His character and dictate how His followers are to act. *Don't lie. Don't take what isn't yours. Don't envy. Don't worship any-thing or anyone besides God.* But trouble comes when we make something into law that God never said was a law or when we think we can perfectly obey the law or when we assume our obedience earns anything from God. When good advice about ironing is elevated to the status of divine law—when we are told that fulfilling a general principle in a very specific way earns God's favor—that good principle is recast as enslaving law. When advice is wedded to God's blessings and curses, the good general truths about overseeing the home become an unnecessary burden. This advice becomes bad law that cannot produce true righteousness in us. It can only produce pride (when we're poised near the dryer with iron in hand) or despair (when we realize that the dryer shut off three hours

Bad Advice WOMEN RECEIVE

What are the dumbest things people tell women they have to do in order to be godly?

(These are real responses to the question I posted on Facebook.)

- Speak quietly and softly, even if you have an outgoing personality.
- Get up early to pray—as if God isn't awake at midnight!
- Have a hard-and-fast time and space for your "quiet time" with God.
- Make sure your quiet time is at least thirty minutes long.
- Get up at five o'clock in the morning and bake your own bread.
- Be the perfect balance of quiet and friendly.
- Be quiet and meek, and do not disagree with your husband or other men.
- Don't laugh out loud. It's too brazen.
- If your child is not following the Lord, it's because

ago and everything in it is now hopelessly wrinkled). We cannot earn anything more from God than what He has already freely given. It isn't that He loves some better, future, more obedient version of us. He loves us as we are *now*.

Here is another example. Have you ever been told that

you have failed in your responsibility of godly parenting.
- If you're sick, it's because you have some kind of sin in your life.
- Don't answer questions in Bible study or Sunday school. Just sit quietly and let the men answer all the questions.
- Refrain from praying in mixed-gender settings.
- Be up before anyone else in your home so you can pray, have a quiet time, and make breakfast for everyone.
- Have food ready when your husband walks through the door.
- You must iron for your husband.
- Don't exhibit a lively sense of humor.
- If your children are disobedient, it's a result of your lack of submission to authority figures in your own life.

THE *Good News*

In him we have redemption through his blood, the forgiveness of our trespasses, according to the riches of his grace.

EPHESIANS 1:7

you need to get up at five in the morning instead of six or eight because five is a godlier hour? (As one woman I heard from said, "As if God isn't awake at midnight!") When people make claims like this, they're twisting the Bible to say more than it actually says. Yes, of course there is a wisdom principle that if I continually sleep in until noon, I'll have trouble finishing the work I need to do—but only because I live in a household with folks who all get up early and I want to be available to connect with them and serve them. (Besides, they wouldn't appreciate hearing me running the vacuum at eleven at night.)

The book of Proverbs does warn about the hazards of laziness (see Proverbs 6:9-11; 19:15; 20:13; 31:15).[18] So, yes, there is a wisdom principle tucked into that advice about rising early, but nowhere in the Bible does it tell me exactly what time I need to get up. And if someone told me that in order to be godly I needed to get up at a certain hour, this would add to the law—something that is clearly prohibited in Scripture (see Deuteronomy 4:2; 12:32).

In 1 Peter 3, Scripture offers instructions for wives who are married to disobedient husbands. They're offered the encouragement that even if their husbands won't listen to their words, they still have an avenue of witness: their godly lives.

> Wives, be subject to your own husbands, so that
> even if some do not obey the word, they may be won
> without a word by the conduct of their wives, when
> they see your respectful and pure conduct. Do not
> let your adorning be external—the braiding of hair
> and the putting on of gold jewelry, or the clothing
> you wear—but let your adorning be the hidden
> person of the heart with the imperishable beauty of
> a gentle and quiet spirit, which in God's sight is very
> precious. For this is how the holy women who hoped

in God used to adorn themselves, by submitting
to their own husbands, as Sarah obeyed Abraham,
calling him lord. And you are her children, if you do
good and do not fear anything that is frightening.

1 PETER 3:1-6

However, this passage has been taken out of context and interpreted to mean everything from "Women should be seen and not heard" to "Women must never wear jewelry." Women have been told that they should have a gentle and quiet *voice*, which is not what the passage says at all. Rather, the passage is a word of hope for women—for those who giggle demurely and for those whose laughter fills the whole room, for those who are shy and don't want to give an opinion and for those who have opinions that they are more than happy to share. It gives women hope that the obedience of their loved ones does not depend on a wife's power to manipulate her husband through words or dress but rather on the Lord—the One in whom they are putting their trust.

Peter's point is not to prohibit a wife's speaking to her
husband about the gospel once he's expressed a lack
of interest in it or opposition to it. His point is that
she has another resource at her disposal, which God
may use instead of spoken witness to break through
her husband's hardness of heart. The real issue is not
whether she ever speaks about her faith to him [or
whether she wears jewelry], but the attitude in which
she does it—in fact, in general, whether he sees in her
the inner beauty of a gentle and quiet spirit.[19]

Here's the good news: the Lord is able to use women's beautiful trust in Him as a way to instruct our loved ones. It's not all up to us to find the right words to say—although this passage does not prohibit our speaking. It is when we rest in the Lord to accomplish His work (with us or without us) that our most beautiful adornment becomes apparent. This adornment, which He says is "very precious," is this: our trust in His grace and power. God doesn't love quiet women more than He loves loud women. God doesn't love women who are makeup free more than He loves women who dress to the nines. When it comes to those He loves, His blessings don't depend on "femininity" as our culture defines it. We can't earn God's love by refraining from voicing our opinions any more than we can earn it by telling everyone we meet what we think.

Women who are extroverts have been made to feel that they are less godly than their introverted sisters, while the truth is that neither shyness nor affability is fundamentally godly. Either one can be used for our own self-protection or self-aggrandizement. And both can be used by the Lord to accomplish His work through us as we rest in His ability to transform lives. Nothing we do can make Him love us more than He already does.

If X Makes God Happy, Then X+Y Must Make Him Really Happy!

Whenever we misinterpret the Bible—when we add to it, contextualize it, don't read it carefully, or fail to recognize the type of literature it is—we become entrapped in the bondage that is always bred by error.[20] Countless women have had their consciences crushed and terrorized by a misapplication of passages. One of the most common ways we misunderstand Scripture is by assuming that if X is a good command, then X+Y must be even better.

Here's an example drawn from the women who responded to my "stupid things" question on Facebook. Many responders said that they have been told that in order to be godly, they and their families should eat only organic food. Now, I live in Southern California, also known as Organic Food Central, so I know what it's like to feel this pressure. Here's how the "If X is good, then X+Y is even better" principle plays out in this case. X = God commands us to care for our bodies and be healthy (inferences drawn from Exodus 20:13 and 1 Corinthians 6:19-20).[21] Therefore, if God would be pleased by our healthy eating, then if we are really, really healthy by doing X+Y, that would make Him even happier.[22] Right?

Please don't misunderstand: if you have the inclination and the resources to shop at Whole Foods stores, have at it—as long as you also have the freedom in your conscience to shop at discount grocers without thinking you've sinned or that God is somehow disappointed in you. Concerns about non-free-range chickens should not be allowed to attack what Luther calls the "kingdom of your conscience,"[23] because all foods and laws concerning food are destined for destruction (see 1 Corinthians 6:13; Colossians 2:21-23; Hebrews 9:9-10). Here is Paul's perspective about the freedom we have in Christ:

One person believes he may eat anything, while
the weak person eats only vegetables. Let not the
one who eats despise the one who abstains, and let
not the one who abstains pass judgment on the one
who eats, for God has welcomed him. . . . Each one
should be fully convinced in his own mind.

ROMANS 14:2-3, 5

Paul's concern is that we do not judge others by what
they eat—in our case, whether they eat organic or not. And
he encourages us not to find our okay-ness either by eating
bean sprouts or by downing chili cheese fries and a quart of
ice cream for dinner. It simply does not make us more or
less godly.

The kind of food we choose to eat is a personal decision
we are free to make. Jesus made this clear when He said,
"'There is nothing outside a person that by going into him
can defile him, but the things that come out of a person are
what defile him. . . . Do you not see that whatever goes into
a person from outside cannot defile him, since it enters not
his heart but his stomach, and is expelled?' (Thus he declared
all foods clean)" (Mark 7:15, 18-19).

Did you catch that? *Jesus declared all foods ceremonially
clean.* That means we have the freedom to choose the foods
to eat and it doesn't affect our standing before God one whit.
Of course, we'll probably feel better and live longer if we
don't eat fried Twinkies all day long, and we'll probably have
more energy to do our work and fulfill our callings if we care
for our bodies and roll off the couch to take a walk from time

to time. But outward conformity to our culture's ideals for health and beauty is completely worthless when it comes to obtaining right standing with God. If that were not the case, Arnold Schwarzenegger would be God's favorite person on the planet.

I know all too well the siren call of "If X is good, then X+Y is better." I've always been told—and I still believe—that there is blessing in reading the Bible every day. I'm thankful I live in a day and a country in which Bibles are so readily available, and I have the various versions of Scripture on my phone, on my tablet, on my computer, and, of course, in hard copies. Generally speaking, I take time nearly every day to read at least one portion of Scripture until I eventually read through an entire book in its context.

But here's the problem: too often I've heard that I need to read a certain number of chapters every day or that I should strive to read the whole Bible in a year in order to please God. As much as I grow and am blessed through reading the Bible, there is no place in Scripture where we're told exactly how many chapters or verses we're supposed to read every day or every year.

The fact is, until Gutenberg developed the printing press and printed the first Bible in the 1450s, very few people even had their own copy. In antiquity few people even saw the biblical manuscripts, and the only ones who were allowed to read them were the religious leaders. For centuries, most biblical manuscripts were written in Latin and kept cloistered in churches. It was many years before the texts became available to the general public, and even then, many people (especially women) were illiterate. The Bible itself wasn't even broken into chapters and verses until the sixteenth century. Even today, some believers, especially those in developing nations or in the persecuted church, have never held an entire New Testament, let alone a whole Bible, during their lifetime. But God is not sitting up in heaven with a frown on His face, unhappy that they didn't check a certain number of verses off their to-do list for the day.

This is another instance where we've acculturated a command to study God's Word to twenty-first-century America and assumed that our norms are God's norms. We've piled so many specific rules about Scripture reading onto God's general command to love His Word that the exhausted mom who falls asleep while trying to keep up on her reading as she nurses her newborn and cares for her toddler assumes that the Lord is disappointed with her. She misses the truth that He sees her and knows what she's going through and rejoices in her desire to love and know Him. The guilt she feels works against her, making her think that God is unhappy with her and stealing from her the desire to be near Him.

Law Multipliers

The practice of adding rules to general principles or making rules more specific than the Bible calls for is nothing new. It began in the Garden of Eden, when both Satan and Eve distorted God's command about the tree of the knowledge of good and evil. God's command was simple: "You may surely eat of every tree of the garden, but of the tree of the

> For a long time I was obsessed with being the perfect submissive wife to my husband. That is what I thought a "noble woman" was according to the Bible. So I obsessed about not inconveniencing him and trying to be a perfect wife who makes dinner, cleans the house, and has sex with him at any time. Trying to be perfect became an idol and robbed both my husband and me of opportunities for growth. Now we are trying to catch up.

knowledge of good and evil you shall not eat, for in the day that you eat of it you shall surely die" (Genesis 2:16-17).

Just a chapter later, that hateful creature, the serpent, came to tempt Eve by making the law include more than just the one prohibited tree. He said, "Did God actually say, 'You shall not eat of any tree in the garden'?" (Genesis 3:1). Already Satan was making the rules sound unreasonable, trying to paint God in a bad light. How were they supposed to live if they couldn't eat from any of the trees? But God didn't say they couldn't eat of *any* of the trees. So Eve corrected him: "We may eat of the fruit of the trees in the garden" (verse 2). But then Eve made her own misapplication of God's command. She broadened it to include an added prohibition: "neither shall you touch it" (verse 3). But the Lord never said that! Satan insinuated that God's rules were too big; Eve countered that His rules weren't big enough. They were both wrong.

As much as we may want to point the finger at Eve here, it's easy to see how she added her own "helpful" rule to God's law. Her reasoning may have gone something like this: If X = you should not eat from the tree of the knowledge of good and evil, then certainly X+Y = you shouldn't touch it either. If X is good, then X+Y must be even better. Right? Of course not! Because just as soon as Eve began to add rules to God's command—to make the law stricter than it actually was— she fell. Perhaps she worried, *What if I accidentally touch the forbidden tree? Wouldn't that be unfair of the Lord to kill me if I just brushed by it? And what if some of the pollen from it falls onto my foot when I walk by? Wouldn't it be mean of Him to kill me for that?*

So when Satan began to blaspheme God's character by telling Eve that God was withholding something good from her and that eating from the tree would actually bring her enlightenment, it wasn't that big a leap for her to eat it and share some of it with her husband, who had been idly standing by, listening to the whole conversation.

I know it may seem counterintuitive, but when we try to make hard-and-fast rules that are more far reaching or more specific than God's law, we are actually opening the door for sin and failure. Why? Because adding to God's law doesn't make it easier to obey; it makes it even more impossible to follow than it already is. We think that adding to the law will make it manageable, but we're terribly mistaken.

If, for instance, your rule is prompt shirt ironing, then when you fail to do so (for whatever reason), you'll begin to complain in your heart about the people who thwarted your good intentions. You'll wonder why your husband has so many stupid shirts you have to iron and why he doesn't get a job that would allow you to send them to the dry cleaner. And speaking of cleaning, you wonder why your husband still hasn't cleaned the garage like he promised. Eventually you even start to complain about the Lord Himself and the unreasonableness of His demands.

Failure to live up to human additions to God's rules always produces guilt, and guilt never produces grateful obedience. Guilt always drives a wedge in our hearts (not God's) between us and Him. Guilt makes us hide from Him and sew together big leaves to cover over our even bigger failures. Guilt makes us unloving and afraid because fear and lovelessness always walk hand in hand.

> There is no fear in love, but perfect love casts out fear. For fear has to do with punishment, and whoever fears has not been perfected in love. We love because he first loved us.   1 JOHN 4:18-19

The fear we experience when we fail does not breed the love we need in order to obey. True obedience must be fueled by love, and love occurs only in hearts that have been warmed by the knowledge of God's love for lawbreakers like us.

Let's go back to our example about being an early-morning

riser or reading a certain amount of Scripture each day. Even if we succeed outwardly in achieving these goals, getting up at five in the morning every day for sixteen years in a row and reading 3.5 chapters of the Bible every day, a day will come when we're unable to do so. Or (and this is worse yet) we might be able to succeed every day but then feel proud of our work and unmerciful toward "sluggards" who don't get up until nine o'clock and never crack open the book once. That lack of love for those who are weak is what Jesus was talking about when He chided those rule multipliers, the Pharisees:

> Those who are well have no need of a physician, but those who are sick. Go and learn what this means, "I desire mercy, and not sacrifice." For I came not to call the righteous, but sinners. MATTHEW 9:12-13

People who foolishly think that they have all their spiritual disciplines together, who assume they're able to obey all the commands (and then some), have a significant problem being merciful with those who struggle. In fact, it was Jesus' adherence to the true meaning of the law and His disdain for the Pharisees' add-ons that made them hate Him. Do you remember the account of Jesus healing a man with a withered hand on the Sabbath? Here's how the outwardly righteous responded: "The Pharisees went out and conspired against [Jesus], how to destroy him" (Matthew 12:14). Why? Because they trusted in themselves; they were proud of their own righteousness. As a result, they viewed everyone else (especially those who didn't comply with their rules and traditions) with contempt (see Luke 18:9-14).

Whenever we add to the law or make it more specific than it actually is, we are headed for failure. Again, that doesn't mean we should shun the helpful advice of the people around us. We just need to make sure we never raise that human advice to the level of God's commands. We must never call anything unclean that He has cleansed; we must never multiply rules in an attempt to make ourselves more "godly."

Not a Cosmic Vending Machine

Now here's where this discussion hits a little closer to home. Sometimes it's not just that we misapply Scripture or are taught misinterpretations about certain passages. Sometimes the trouble comes from within our own hearts. We need to do an honest self-evaluation to determine whether we are relying on any good deed, whatever that good deed might be, to earn God's blessing.

If, for instance, you believe that choosing to home-school your children will automatically ensure that they will always love you and follow God, you are expecting too much from your own work. I'm not saying that homeschooling your children isn't a good choice for your family; I'm saying that all human efforts will fall short of transforming anyone's heart. The truth is that we can't transform our own hearts, let alone anyone else's. That's something only the Lord can do.

God is not a cosmic vending machine. He doesn't display a row of buttons that light up when we put forth the right effort. But even though this idea is antithetical to the gospel, many Christians believe that if we put in the right nickel, God is obliged to bless us with a prosperous life.

This is the same error Job's "comforters" believed. They were convinced that good things happen to good people and that bad things happen only to bad people. This is what Eliphaz meant when he said, "As I have seen, those who plow iniquity and sow trouble reap the same" (Job 4:8). Another friend named Zophar launched this accusation against Job: "The exulting of the wicked is short, and the joy of the godless but for a moment. . . . He will perish forever like his own dung" (Job 20:5, 7).

These words sound as if they should be right . . . at least according to the principle of karma. But we know they are not the truth. It's clear from the beginning of the book that Job was not suffering because he was unrighteous but rather because he was particularly righteous and the Lord wanted to show off Job's faith to Satan, who had been blaspheming Him. Scripture makes it clear that Job's friends' this-for-that mentality, their what-goes-around-comes-around perspective, was faulty. Here is God's rebuke against them:

> My anger burns against you and against your two
> friends, for you have not spoken of me what is right,
> as my servant Job has. . . . My servant Job shall pray
> for you, for I will accept his prayer not to deal with
> you according to your folly. For you have not spoken
> of me what is right, as my servant Job has.
>
> JOB 42:7-8

The Source OF THE BAD NEWS

Where does the bad news for women come from?

(The following responses were gathered from focus groups.)

- Competitiveness among women
- Myself—comparing myself to other women
- The media
- Social media—people post only the good stuff
- Workplace and the pressure to perform
- Some conservative pastors and Christian leaders
- Scripture (either correctly or incorrectly interpreted)
- Conferences that emphasize motherhood
- Pinterest (look at all these amazing things I should be doing!), Facebook (look how happy her family is!), Instagram (comparing myself to others)
- Well-intentioned Christian women
- Christian books, speakers, and blogs
- The enemy
- My own heart

THE Good News

[The Lord] does not deal with us according to our sins,
nor repay us according to our iniquities.
For as high as the heavens are above the earth,
so great is his steadfast love toward those who fear him;
as far as the east is from the west,
so far does he remove our transgressions from us.

PSALM 103:10-12

If God is not a cosmic vending machine, and if there's no guaranteed equation that obedience equals blessings, then how *should* we think about His laws? It comes down to this: we can't grasp the law without an understanding of grace.

Law and Grace

In the Old Testament, God spelled out His law for living in communion with Him, along with the blessings of obedience and the curses that came along with disobedience. He told His people that they would know great blessing in the land He was giving them if they faithfully obeyed all His commands. He formalized and summarized His moral instructions in Exodus 20, where they are listed for us as the Ten Commandments. The blessings for obedience and the curses for disobedience are clearly spelled out in Deuteronomy 28. But of course God's people failed to obey.

You see, their obedience problem wasn't something they could solve by mere good intentions or extra elbow grease. They would never be able to overcome their difficulty with the law, because they had a heart problem. The Lord said that they had a "foreskin" on their hearts that needed to be cut away. They were stubborn and disobedient by nature, and the only way they could achieve victory over sin was if God did something for them that they could never do for themselves.

"Circumcise therefore the foreskin of your heart," God commanded, "and be no longer stubborn" (Deuteronomy 10:16). Wait . . . what? How were they supposed to do that? In some ways this command is analogous to Jesus' telling Nicodemus he had to be "born again." Nicodemus's response was appropriate: "How can a man be born when he is old? Can he enter a second time into his mother's womb and be born?" (John 3:4). If we view God's law as something we can fulfill, we're not understanding it right. The only way for the people of Israel to overcome their stubborn disobedience was to have a change in their nature. Their old nature—their flesh—had to be cut away by the Spirit of God. They couldn't do that on their own, and neither can we. Someone has to step in and do it for us . . . and the good news is that He already has!

In case you're still not convinced that, like Israel, we are unable to circumcise our own hearts, be born again, and change our own nature, here are the merciful and gracious words of the Lord to His disobedient people:

> The LORD your God will circumcise your heart and
> the heart of your offspring, so that you will love the
> LORD your God with all your heart and with all your
> soul, that you may live.   DEUTERONOMY 30:6

How would the people respond to His law? God knew even before He gave them the land what they would do:

> When I have brought them into the land flowing
> with milk and honey, which I swore to give to their
> fathers, and they have eaten and are full and grown
> fat, they will turn to other gods and serve them, and
> despise me and break my covenant. . . . For I know

what they are inclined to do even today, before I
have brought them into the land that I swore to give.

DEUTERONOMY 31:20-21

All the laws in Scripture—the instructions in the Old
Testament, the commandments summarized by Christ in the
New Testament (see Matthew 22:37), and all the obligations
given to us in the Epistles—are given for one primary reason:
to make it clear to our hard, proud, and all-too-confident
hearts that we can't do it. The law is also there to make us
grateful for Christ's perfect keeping of the law in our place.
Finally, it's there to show us what grateful obedience and love
for God and our neighbor should look like.

But it should be obvious by now that our keeping of the
law is not something we're able to do on our own. When
it comes to our standing before God, our law keeping does
not influence His blessing on us one bit. As Martin Luther
wrote in his commentary on the book of Galatians, "God
does not slack his promises because of our sins . . . or has-
ten them because of our righteousness and merits. He pays
no attention to either."[24] In other words, we don't earn His
promised blessings by successfully marking things off our
to-do lists.

Keeping Mom's Advice Where It Belongs

As I've said, I am thankful for the advice I've received from
women over the years. But all those tips for a good life need
to be weighed carefully and kept away from the kingdom of
my conscience. We will experience joy and freedom when we

can learn to recognize laws that have been made too broad or multiplied too specifically. In addition, if we remember that God's law has already been fulfilled by Jesus Christ, who obeyed in our place and then died for all our disobedience, we will grow in our desire to love Him and live for Him—not out of obligation but out of gratitude for His mercy.

So iron those shirts . . . or don't! Eat acai berry–laced gluten-free pancakes . . . or don't. Get up at 4:17 a.m. to do your devotions . . . or don't. The Lord has given you the freedom to seek to serve Him in whatever way He has wired you to. And then, in all the ways you fail, He also gives you His righteousness.

Questions FOR REFLECTION AND DISCUSSION

1. Martin Luther wrote, "The foolishness of the human heart is so great that in this conflict of conscience, when the law has done what it is supposed to do, we not only lay hold on the doctrine of grace, which promises forgiveness of sins for Christ's sake, but we seek more laws to satisfy our conscience."[25] How has your heart been foolish in seeking more laws in an attempt to satisfy your conscience?

2. What are some of the "multiplied" rules you've heard that supposedly make God happier with you?

3. What rules have you embraced that plague your conscience now? Are these laws biblical, or have they been added on to Scripture?

4. How would it change your perspective to realize that when God sees you, He looks at Christ's record of perfect obedience? How would this change the way you view your own failures?

5. Summarize what you've learned in this chapter in four or five sentences.

CHAPTER 4

WHEN RULES
DEFINE YOU

I RECENTLY SPOKE at a women's conference, and afterward I received an e-mail from one of the women in attendance. Angela had resonated with my message about the gospel of grace, and she sent me this story about her journey from rules to freedom:

> I learned at a young age to pretend everything was fine. When I was growing up, there was a lot of conflict at home, and everything was not fine. But my family always pretended we had it all together. I made up my mind to not live like this when I grew up and got married someday. I would submit to my husband, whatever that meant, and not argue with him.

I was a very agreeable child, trying to earn others' approval. I learned to be a good pretender. Because I was so set on avoiding conflict, I made all my decisions based on what other people thought I should do. It was work, work, work all the time to try to gain their acceptance.

This dangerous pattern led me to marry a man who had a clear idea of what he wanted from a woman, and I was the perfect doormat to meet his every whim. Just a few weeks into the marriage, I realized I would never be able to meet the demands of the tyrant I had married. I felt like I was failing, and I became depressed.

I'd thought this was what I wanted—someone who would tell me what to do and then say, "Good job—you did exactly what I asked." Well, I soon discovered that when you have a tyrant and a doormat in a relationship together, the result is all kinds of abuse.

When I got pregnant, I thought, *Things will be better now—I'll have someone else to live for. I can just check out of my miserable marriage and focus on my baby.* But I was still conscious after she was born, and I was stuck in a life I couldn't escape. Not only that, but I didn't want my little girl to grow up in the same abusive cycle I was experiencing.

Three months after my daughter was born, I ran for my life. I am now remarried to a man who loves Jesus and cares for my daughter as his own. But I will never be able to undo the pain that was caused during those treacherous years—for me and for my daughter.

Everywhere we turn, we are confronted with rules, steps, lists, and seemingly benign advice that function as deadly law. For some of us, like Angela, the pressure to meet these impossible expectations can make us feel as if our boat has suddenly capsized. For others, it feels more like we're experiencing a slow leak. Either way, we're struggling to stay afloat—and we're growing weary.

When I take my grandchildren to playgrounds, I feel much sympathy for the moms who are there with their children. Gone are the days when a tired mama could take her kiddies to the park to ride swings for a few hours while she relaxes and enjoys a little sunshine (and hopefully doesn't fall asleep), like I used to. Now the demands on mothers have increased exponentially.

Before a child even enters the playground, Mom has to disinfect every surface. She has to be vigilant to guard against playground equipment that isn't up to code, snacks with high-fructose corn syrup, and would-be predators. And when it comes to the strollers and recreational vehicles kids ride around in—well, let's just say I've considered going back to school and getting an engineering degree so I can assemble and disassemble them for my grandchildren. Women are trying to build a completely safe (death-free) environment in a sin-cursed, death-riddled world, and it's exhausting.

Bad Advice WOMEN RECEIVE

***What are the dumbest things people tell women they
have to do in order to be godly?***

(These are real responses to the question I posted on
Facebook.)

- Never disagree with other people—especially not
  your husband.
- Always, always obey the law!
- Only listen to Christian music.
- Only read Christian books (or books with a strong
  Christian moral).
- Only have natural birth. Homeschool your children.
  Eat organic foods.
- Always submit—followed by a terrible definition
  of the word.
- Never drink beer, wine, or any kind of alcohol (even
  in moderation).

Moms also feel pressure to make sure their children are
learning and growing, both academically and socially—no
more simple, unplanned playtimes. Moms are expected
to sign their kids up for dance classes, music classes, and
reading-enrichment programs when their kids are as young
as possible so they won't fall behind. Their whole day is to be
regimented and scheduled down to the minute.

Under the rubric of wisdom and appropriate use of time,
it's a good idea to protect children from real danger and to be

- Shop at Hobby Lobby, not Michaels, since they play Christian music at Hobby Lobby.
- Don't go to yoga class at the gym.
- Don't allow your children to be exposed to Disney characters.
- Godliness means you have to vote a certain way.
- Godliness means you have to boycott places that support gay rights.
- Stay with an abusive husband even if you feel threatened.
- When your children misbehave, you should be able to quote verses to them (or have them recite verses to you).

THE *Good News*

[Jesus said,] "Come to me, all who labor and are heavy laden, and I will give you rest. Take my yoke upon you, and learn from me, for I am gentle and lowly in heart, and you will find rest for your souls. For my yoke is easy, and my burden is light." MATTHEW 11:28-30

intentional about the activities they're involved in. It's a no-brainer that it's unwise to allow secondhand smoke into your kids' lungs, and you don't want little Fiona munching on cat feces from the public sandbox. On the other hand, when our focus on germs, UV rays, self-esteem, and secondhand smoke becomes an obsession, we start to go beyond what Scripture says. These rules mean too much to us; they have become too important. Rather than give us peace of mind, they cause separations, cliques, factions, and disunity.

Our Laws Define Us

Whether we're aware of it or not, we all define ourselves by the rules or laws we keep. We tend to hang around with people who have the same standards we do. One of the primary ways we construct our identity and answer the question "Who am I?" is through lists, steps, and laws. When we say that we have a lot in common with someone, we don't just mean they have the same interests we do—we also mean they obey similar rules. We tend to have a narrow definition of what it means to be a "good Christian woman," and we fail to realize that our definition might look completely different for another Christian woman who is loved by God just as much as we are.

If you wonder whether you're defining yourself by your own lists, here's a quick gut check: Do you have friends who hold to different standards than you do? For instance, do you have any friends who vote differently or observe different rules about alcohol or make different decisions about their children's schooling? Do you catch yourself saying things like, "I would never do that! I mean, I might do X, but I would never do Y"? Or maybe you've said, "I can't believe she lets her kids eat *that*!" Or "Wow, she never should have watched that movie!" Or "Can you believe she posted that picture on Facebook?" It's true that we are not to be yoked with unbelievers (see 2 Corinthians 6:14). But we need to make allowance for areas where Scripture is open to interpretation and Christians can legitimately disagree (see Romans 14:1-12).

So if these rules that consume us aren't found in Scripture, where do they come from? Many of them are imposed on us by our parents and our upbringing. We also pick them up from other family members or from our friends. Sometimes we get them from books or the Internet. Then there are the News Nannies, who tell us how to live by informing us of another taxpayer-funded study. Their report begins with a warning like this: "A study of 2,500 children who ate candy bars for lunch every day has shown. . . ." By the time they're finished, we have at least one more brick to add to our backpacks, which are already full of advice about what we must do to be a good mother.

No matter where these standards originated, once a rule has taken root in our hearts, it is nearly impossible to extract it, especially if it came with some sort of promise of reward or threat of punishment. If we believe that God is pleased by our rule keeping, we will find it difficult to abandon those rules without feeling guilty and fearing that something bad will happen to us if we don't comply.

The reason we define ourselves by rules is that we are all, by nature, legalists. We love rules. They make us feel safe and in control, and they offer a means by which we can approve of ourselves and achieve perfection. But we have a serious problem: we are also, by nature, rule breakers. That means that even though we may pride ourselves on keeping certain rules, we are hopelessly inconsistent. The more inconsistent we are, the harder we'll work at becoming consistent—and the more driven we become to pedal faster and try harder.

Yet we will always fail. As long as we're looking to ourselves for safety, approval, and perfection, our consciences will never be silenced. We will never experience freedom from the tyranny of rules until Christ has been crowned King of our lives, until He has banished all our efforts at self-perfection, self-protection, and self-justification. There is only one way for rule breakers like us to achieve perfection: with His perfect life lived in our place.

The Laws We Break

The Gospel of John records a conversation Jesus had with the immoral woman of Samaria. It offers a striking example of the way we are prone to define ourselves by the law, even though we don't keep it ourselves.

In this story, an unnamed woman drew water from Jacob's well in the afternoon. Most women of her time would have drawn water in the morning, so the fact that she was there later in the day implies that she didn't hang around the other women, who kept the laws about men and decency. Perhaps this woman had been ostracized by them, or perhaps she had ostracized herself. In any case, she had no girlfriends to walk to the well with, and it seems evident that she had been shunned by her community.

But Jesus was not put off by her tarnished reputation:

Jesus said to her, "Give me a drink." (For his disciples had gone away into the city to buy food.) The Samaritan woman said to him, "How is it that you, a Jew, ask for a drink from me, a woman of Samaria?" (For Jews have no dealings with Samaritans.) JOHN 4:7-9

Think of it: here's an immoral woman questioning Jesus about the rules. She'd had five husbands, and she hadn't even taken vows with the fellow she was currently living with. Elizabeth Taylor might as well have been giving Queen Elizabeth lessons on a proper marriage. Yet this woman questioned Jesus about His laws for worship:

> The woman said to him, "Sir, I perceive that you are a prophet. Our fathers worshiped on this mountain, but you say that in Jerusalem is the place where people ought to worship." JOHN 4:19-20

The Samaritans didn't believe they needed to go up to Jerusalem to worship God, as the Jews did. Instead, they worshiped at Mount Gerizim, a local mountain where they had historically mixed the worship of Yahweh with idols.

So why would this woman, a lawbreaker and a Samaritan, want to talk to Jesus about the rules? I think she went there because rules are safe to discuss. "We are allergic to grace. We resist it. Like this woman, we look for ways to avoid Jesus" and His pursuit of our hearts.[26] Kibitzing about "correct rules" is one of our favorite topics—especially if we want to deflect the focus off our personal failures. We may be tempted to point a finger at the Samaritan woman, but we do the same thing. We hide behind our rules and use them to make us feel superior to others. They also take the focus off our flawed rule keeping and the discomfort inherent in grace. They make us think that if we could just find the right rules to keep, we'd be okay. Of course, we're wrong.

When the disciples returned to Sychar with lunch for the Lord, they were astonished that He would sully Himself by talking to a Samaritan woman with loose morals. They didn't know who they were dealing with—and neither do we.

Jesus is the only One who never defined Himself by rules He failed to keep. Instead of being enslaved by man-made laws, He crashed right through every cultural boundary. He was more interested in having relationships than He was in punctiliously complying with every man-made rule and tradition. In fact, He associated with rule breakers so frequently that He brought scorn upon Himself from religious people who built their identity on the rules.

Jesus associated with prostitutes, gluttons, tax collectors, and drunkards, but He never became one Himself. Since His identity was rooted in His relationship with His Father, not in outward conformity to the law, He wasn't worried about being contaminated by people's sin. He never built walls between Himself and the unclean because His holiness was comprehensive enough to transform lawbreakers into law keepers.

Jesus' love for lawbreakers had a lasting effect on other people too. After His ascension, Peter and John went back to Samaria—not to judge this time but to bring the Samaritans the good news:

> When they had testified and spoken the word of the Lord, they returned to Jerusalem, preaching the gospel to many villages of the Samaritans. ACTS 8:25

The biggest false message I've received about becoming the woman God wants me to be—and maybe the most damaging at its root—is that I should be self-sufficient. In the years I've been a Christian, I've gotten the impression that I shouldn't need anyone or anything—or at least I should be able to take care of my own needs. I shouldn't be dependent on other people for help. And for a long time, this included God. I would have said I needed Him for salvation, but I lived for many years under the belief that as I grew in Christ and became a more mature Christian, I would need God less. I needed to try to sin less, to get my own stuff under control, until eventually I would get to the point where I would no longer need Him in my daily life. I'm starting to understand, though, that we never outgrow our need for God and our dependence on Him. It's grace that saves us and grace that keeps us.

These disciples, who had once found their identity in the law that separated them from the Samaritans, had been transformed. They had learned how to love; they had found their identity in the only One who can perfectly keep the law. They had learned to see themselves as they really were: run-of-the-mill sinners who were loved by a perfect Man.

Breaking Down Walls

In the early years of the church, a debate raged among the disciples. The question was whether the Gentiles who had come to Christ were obliged to obey Israel's ceremonial laws. The disciples of Jewish origin, who had sought their identity in the law for their entire lives, must have found this a confusing and terrifying time.

Imagine spending several decades thinking you had to do certain things in order to please God, only to learn that God was already smiling on you—as a result of your faith alone. All those years they'd spent trying to keep the rules hadn't profited them at all. And then they learned that God showed His favor to the Gentiles, too, welcoming them with no prerequisites but merely on the terms of their faith in Him. Talk about having your world turned upside down!

As a good Hebrew, Peter had built his identity on his compliance with the Old Testament dietary laws (see Leviticus 11). So when Peter had a vision in which the Lord told him to "rise . . . kill and eat" various animals (Acts 10:13) such as reptiles and birds (which would have been considered forbidden by Jewish standards), Peter objected. "By no means, Lord; for I have never eaten anything that is common or unclean" (verse 14).

The laws Peter observed made him believe that he merited special favor with God. He thought God smiled on him because he didn't eat ham. But he was wrong. Yes, God loved him, but it wasn't because of his lunch menu. And—news flash—He loved those who ate pork, too! God was about to teach Peter a powerful lesson—a lesson that was broader than rules about what kinds of sandwiches he could eat.

The Lord said, "What God has made clean, do not call common" (Acts 10:15). Apart from setting aside the dietary laws of the Old Testament, the Lord was also saying that the laws Peter assumed made him superior to others were ineffective in earning God's blessing. God was declaring that the Gentiles were welcome at His table, that all people were precious to Him. He wanted a relationship with everyone, and this relationship would be based on His Son's perfect keeping of the law and on His people's faith in Him, not on their determination to keep a kosher house.

God knew that as long as Peter defined himself by rules, he would never be able to love his Gentile sisters and brothers. He would always look down on them. He had to grasp that God didn't love him because of any good rule keeping on his part. The Lord loved him out of His free grace—grace that Peter needed just as the Gentiles did.

Before Peter's eyes were opened by the Lord, he believed it was "unlawful" for him to "associate with or to visit anyone of another nation" (Acts 10:28). Where did he get that idea? It wasn't from God. It was a man-made tradition—a classic case of "If X is good, then X+Y must be better." The Israelites wanted to obey the command not to worship foreign gods or marry foreign wives who would lead them to worship idols, so they made extra rules about associating with and eating with foreigners. The irony was that in doing so, they transgressed commandments about loving their neighbors and showing kindness to strangers. But X+Y made them feel safe and entitled and extra-holy.

When the Lord told Peter to "kill and eat," God was breaking down the wall that had separated Jews and Gentiles, the wall that religious people had set up to make themselves feel superior to everyone else. In Ephesians 2, Paul talks about the hostility between Jews and Gentiles:

> In Christ Jesus you who once were far off have
> been brought near by the blood of Christ. For he
> himself is our peace, who has made us both one
> and has broken down in his flesh the dividing wall
> of hostility *by abolishing the law of commandments
> expressed in ordinances*, that he might create in
> himself one new man in place of the two, so making
> peace, and might reconcile us both to God in one
> body through the cross, thereby killing the hostility.
> EPHESIANS 2:13-16 *(emphasis added)*

What was the dividing wall between Jew and Gentile? It's the same thing that creates hostility between us and others—those to-do lists, laws, rules, and steps that we elevate to utmost importance. But those rules we create in an attempt to earn God's favor only end up setting us apart from others. As Christians, we are to be defined not by rules but rather by the One who fulfilled the law on our behalf and then died for us while we were still lawbreakers.

Where We Find Our Identity

Saul (later called Paul) was a proud rule keeper too. His adherence to the traditions of his nation and religion defined his identity and made him hate everyone who sought a relationship with God apart from the traditions of the Pharisees. In his letters to the early churches, he describes his life before he encountered Christ:

> You are familiar with all the customs and controversies of the Jews. . . . My manner of life from my youth, spent from the beginning among my own nation and in Jerusalem . . . that according to the strictest party of our religion I have lived as a Pharisee. . . . I myself was convinced that I ought to do many things in opposing the name of Jesus of Nazareth. And I did so in Jerusalem. I not only locked up many of the saints in prison after receiving authority from the chief priests, but when they were put to death I cast my vote against them. And I punished them often in all the synagogues and tried to make them blaspheme, and in raging fury against them I persecuted them even to foreign cities. ACTS 26:3-5, 9-11

> You have heard of my former life in Judaism, how I persecuted the church of God violently and tried to destroy it. And I was advancing in Judaism beyond many of my own age among my people, so extremely zealous was I for the traditions of my fathers.
> GALATIANS 1:13-14

THE *Guilt Trips* WE PLACE ON OURSELVES

What do you feel guilty about?

(The following responses were gathered from focus groups.)

- Spending time with friends when I should be with my family
- Making time for myself
- Not cooking real meals
- Spending money on myself (I don't feel worthy)
- Not being able to meet everyone's needs
- Seeking independence when I should be willing to accept help
- Not keeping in touch with my extended family
- Forgetting to return calls and e-mails
- Not saving money well or investing wisely
- Wasting my twenties and feeling like I have nothing to show for it
- Sexual desires
- Past sins
- Not always super prepared for the week ahead
- Not sticking to the budget
- Not being enough for my kids and my husband
- Failing over and over
- Not pleasing other people
- Eating too much sugar
- Needing too much grace

- Sending unhealthy snacks to school
- Spending too much money on groceries
- Being overweight
- Yelling at my kids
- Wanting time away from my kids
- Not being the perfect wife, perfect employee, perfect Christian, perfect neighbor, perfect superwoman
- Having clutter in my home
- Not meeting people's expectations
- Feeling jealous of others
- Not getting enough done during the day
- Not appreciating the small moments with my kids each day
- Not having kids
- Not being more available to my husband
- Not reading my Bible enough and not praying enough
- Not reading to my kids enough
- Not creating enough special memories with our kids
- Not exercising enough
- Not being enough

THE Good News

God shows his love for us in that while we were still sinners, Christ died for us. Since, therefore, we have now been justified by his blood, much more shall we be saved by him from the wrath of God. ROMANS 5:8-9

What was Saul's problem with Christianity? It threatened his supposed superior place as a rule-keeping son. Saul's entire identity was wrapped up in his fastidious execution of the rules, so the Lord had to knock him off his high horse and blind him before he was willing to give up his self-righteous identity and his allegiance to his own rules. Paul would later become the foremost spokesman for grace—but only after he came to the realization that his okay-ness, his righteousness according to the law, was worthless. In his letter to the Philippians, Paul wrote, "I count everything as loss . . . and count [all things] as rubbish, in order that I may gain Christ" (Philippians 3:8).

Paul knew that even though he had prided himself on outward obedience to the law, he had not actually obeyed it—at least not from the heart, as the law demanded (see Romans 2 and 7). It wasn't until his encounter with the risen Christ that Paul saw himself as he really was. He was a sinner in need of righteousness that could not come from his own effort—just as we are.

What Should We Boast About?

Later in Paul's life, after he had completely embraced the free pardon and righteousness given to him by the Lord, he, too, faced persecution from the super-rule-following religious types. In Corinth some were saying he wasn't a real apostle; they said his speech was flawed and that he was weak (see 2 Corinthians 10:10).

In response, much of the letter of 2 Corinthians was written as a defense of the ministry Christ had given him.

However, Paul defended himself in an unusual way: by pointing out the work God had accomplished through his suffering and his weakness. Paul refused to be drawn into a boasting war with his detractors unless what he could boast about was his weaknesses. He simply refused to enter into the folly of trying to approve of himself or prove his worth in the eyes of people. He said, "Not that we dare to . . . compare ourselves with some of those who are commending themselves. But when they measure themselves by one another and compare themselves with one another, they are without understanding" (2 Corinthians 10:12).

It's shocking, isn't it, that the man whose complete identity had once been wrapped up in his own résumé had been so transformed by grace that he called the pursuit of self-commendation foolishness?

The desire to brag about our accomplishments, especially to ourselves, is rooted deep within our hearts. Thousands of years ago, the prophet Jeremiah spoke about this universal craving:

> Let not the wise man boast in his wisdom, let not
> the mighty man boast in his might, let not the rich
> man boast in his riches, but let him who boasts boast
> in this, that he understands and knows me, that I
> am the LORD who practices steadfast love, justice,
> and righteousness in the earth. For in these things
> I delight.   JEREMIAH 9:23-24

Let's take a moment for some self-reflection. What do you boast in? Do you boast in your abilities or your wisdom or your nice home or your mad parenting skills? What gives you assurance and confidence at the end of the day? Are you pleased with yourself because you have your theological ducks in a row or because you're involved in all sorts of worthy causes?

If we are tempted to boast about something, we can follow Paul's example and boast about our weaknesses. I can't think of many things more countercultural than such an approach. Rather than boasting (even in our own hearts) about our superiority, our great accomplishments, or our diligent labor, we see that the pattern set in Scripture is to boast about our "weaknesses, so that the power of Christ may rest upon [us]" (2 Corinthians 12:9).

It seems to me that the whole point of all the steps, lists, and bad advice we're given is to overcome any sense of weakness. That message sells because we don't want to appear weak in our own eyes—or in anyone else's. We've forgotten the truth that Paul knew: "When I am weak, then I am strong" (2 Corinthians 12:10).

The Lord's word to you and to me is simply this: don't boast in anything you do or anything you have. Boast only in the truth that you are loved by the Lord, who poured out His just wrath on your Savior and clothed you in His righteousness. Don't seek to commend yourself, because "it is not the one who commends himself who is approved, but the one whom the Lord commends" (2 Corinthians 10:18). And the really wonderful but all-too-often overlooked truth is that the Lord already commends you. Not for those things you think are commendable, but for the sake of the Son He loves.

The Law of Love

Jesus summarized the entire law in these words:

> You shall love the Lord your God with all your heart
> and with all your soul and with all your mind. This
> is the great and first commandment. And a second is
> like it: You shall love your neighbor as yourself. On
> these two commandments depend all the Law and
> the Prophets.   MATTHEW 22:37-40

This is the law we are called to obey—the law of love—
and yet when we think about it, it's the one thing none of us
can do perfectly or consistently—no matter how hard we try.
None of us love our neighbors as we should, and all the steps,
lists, and advice we receive, no matter how well intentioned,
can never transform our hearts. In fact, this advice actually
causes us to stumble and build walls of separation between us
and our pork-eating, wine-drinking, public-school-attending
sisters and brothers.

Is there any hope for us? Yes, of course. That hope is
found in the good news:

> *All the law you must obey has been obeyed by Jesus*
> *in your place.*
> *All the sins you have committed have been washed*
> *away in His blood.*

You are free now from all the to-do lists, steps, bad advice,
and traditions you once relied on to make yourself feel okay
and to elevate yourself above others. You are free to love

sinners because you have been loved. You are free to forgive sinners because you have been forgiven. All the walls of separation between you and the unruly folks down the street have been torn down. You are now free to see yourself as you really are and to love others as they really are. All because of His love and His perfect keeping of the law in your place.

Questions FOR REFLECTION AND DISCUSSION

1. Galatians 2:15-16 says, "We ourselves are Jews by birth and not Gentile sinners; yet we know that a person is not justified by works of the law but through faith in Jesus Christ, so we also have believed in Christ Jesus, in order to be justified by faith in Christ and not by works of the law, because by works of the law no one will be justified." What does this passage say about everyone who seeks to be made right with God? What does this passage say about our ability to be made right through the law?

2. Even though Peter had been commanded by God not to view himself as better than the Gentiles, he fell back into his old ways in Galatia. That's when Paul opposed him because his "conduct was not in step with the truth of the gospel" (see Galatians 2:11-14). In what ways have you judged others or disassociated yourself from them because they didn't keep the same rules or traditions as you?

3. Can you think of any way that you try to prevent others from seeing your weaknesses? Could you say with Paul that you are "content with weaknesses, insults, hardships, persecutions, and calamities" (2 Corinthians 12:10)? What do you think about the idea that you are strong at the very point of your weakness?

4. Author and theologian John T. Pless says, "The Gospel is not a recipe for self-improvement."[27] What do you think this means? How does Scripture back up this idea?

5. Summarize what you've learned in this chapter in four or five sentences.

CHAPTER 5

THE DELUSION OF SELF-PERFECTION

EARLY ON IN MY LIFE, people told me that although I had gifts, I also had a bent toward pride. They warned me that this was something I needed to keep in check. I'd like to say I took that advice to heart and immediately became humble, but every time I tried to be humble, I found myself becoming proud about it—and then feeling proud of my self-awareness. There were stretches of time when I gave up the fight and figured that my problem wasn't really a pride issue; I just had a lot of confidence because, after all, I was right. Other times I learned catchphrases that sounded humble, and I inserted them whenever I could to prove that I had an attitude of humility. It didn't help. As C. S. Lewis wrote, "A man is never so proud as when striking an attitude of humility."[28]

I'd like to say that my struggle with pride ended early in my Christian walk. But the truth is, I continued to struggle with it for decades—and in some ways, I still do.

When I was a young mom, I was privileged to teach in a Christian school. I taught Bible, art, yearbook, and home economics courses to junior and senior high students. I really enjoyed teaching the Bible to those young hearts, and I was also happy that this job meant our children would have free tuition. But there was one problem: I was very proud of the work I was doing.

On one particular evening, the parents and students were gathered together for an end-of-the-year gala. Part of the agenda for the evening was a time for the administrator to talk about each staff member. The room was packed, and everyone was dressed up. I was sure I was going to hear good things about all the hard work I had done. But our administrator had another thought in mind. When it was time to talk about me, he made jokes about how pots and pans had been flying all over the kitchen and how we'd been making a mess in my home economics classes. Looking back now, I'm sure he didn't mean to insult me. But because I was proud and eager to hear my own praises sung, I was insulted—crushed, even. I cried all the way home.

In my anger and humiliation, I considered quitting my job. I spoke unkindly about the administration. And while no one likes to receive criticism, especially in public, my pride had made me hypersensitive to criticism. My overreaction was the fruit of a heart that trusted in my own goodness and abilities. I wrongly thought my identity was defined by my work and other people's approval of it. I was wrong.

I wish I could say this was the only time something like this has happened to me, but it isn't. The truth is, I continually struggle with the desire to gain people's respect. In some ways this desire has lessened as I've grown in my understanding of who I am in Christ, but in other areas it's still there. The only way I've found to kill that desire for human approval is the good news of the gospel: yes, I am sinful and flawed, but I am also loved and welcomed. It doesn't really matter what other people say or do. God loves me, even in my brokenness, and that's all that matters.

If you are looking for the secret to perfection so you won't sin every day, I don't have any helpful hints for you. The one thing I've learned—the sole piece of advice I have to offer—is that you shouldn't look to me or to any other flawed human being, but rather to the only One who justifies you through His life, death, and resurrection. And I should add that even when we believe in Him, we'll never follow Him consistently, perfectly, or with our whole hearts. We'll continue to hope for secrets or tricks to make ourselves better. This deluded optimism is in our DNA—it's been there since we decided to take our godliness into our own hands in the Garden (see Genesis 3).

I've come to realize that there is only one way out of this kind of thinking: I need to give up all my efforts at being humble and throw myself on the mercy of Christ. All I can do is go to Him for mercy over and over and over again. As Lewis once said, trying to attack pride in your own heart is like fighting the Hydra, that mythical creature with numerous heads—it's a futile, unending war you're guaranteed to lose. He described our plight as "depth under depth of self-love and self-admiration."[29]

Either "I'm Better Than You!" or "I'm Such a Failure!"

I've spent a significant portion of my life alternating between feeling superior to others and feeling like a complete failure. These feelings flow out of my pride and my inveterate belief that I'm better than my record demonstrates.

There are certain areas of my life where I've been so proud of my ability to achieve my goals that I've become impatient and unkind toward others who don't meet my standards. There are other areas where I fail incessantly— and I know it.

God has blessed me with a wonderful husband, three children, and six adorable grandchildren. As of this writing, my mother, who is ninety-one, is still with us. These dear people are a sweet source of blessing to me, but they are also the impetus for significant sin in my life. I've been angry, self-pitying, covetous, judgmental, demanding, selfish, and unkind (at least in my heart) every day of my life. I haven't loved people as I should, but I've expected them to faithfully love me as they should. I've said things and thought things about them that are unkind and even horrific at times. I haven't been consistently faithful to them. I haven't loved them perfectly. I've been demanding with them.

My husband worked selflessly to provide for our family

for decades, but I wasn't as grateful toward him as I should have been. I interpreted his faithful love and willingness to serve as weakness, and I nagged him to be more assertive and to stand up for his rights (read: my demands).

And then there's my relationship with the Lord. I've been blessed with the knowledge of His presence for more than forty years now. I've been given His Word, His Spirit, His pardon, and His comfort. I've been given His grace and His mercy. I've been granted a ministry that reaches far beyond my expectations, and our family has been blessed through it. I've read the testimonies of countless women (and men) whose lives have been transformed by God through my work.

And yet, oh my heart, I do not trust Him yet. Yes, I trust Him right now, as I'm writing this, but when I wake up in the middle of the night or when things aren't going the way I think they should, I don't trust Him. I don't trust that He has everything worked out for my good. I don't believe, so I complain. Listen, I live in San Diego, the one city on the planet with nearly perfect weather, and I complain about that, too.

When I dig down deeper, I realize that my complaining is inextricably tied to my pride. I think I deserve better, and even though I say out loud that I deserve hell (one of my humble-sounding catchphrases), my complaining portrays a different picture of my heart. I think I deserve heaven in the here and now.

I'm not saying all this because confession is good for the soul or because I want you to tell me I'm really not that bad after all or because I'm feigning humility. No, I'm saying it because I want you to know that I struggle the way

Bad Advice WOMEN RECEIVE

What are the dumbest things people tell women they have to do in order to be godly?

(These are real responses to the question I posted on Facebook.)

- Always have a clean, orderly home.
- Don't wear jewelry or make yourself look too good, because otherwise you'll become prideful.
- If your children disobey or are strong willed, it's because you're not a godly mom.
- You shouldn't waste time on Facebook.
- Godliness is shown in things like how organized your closet is, because God is a God of order.
- It is selfish and sinful to stay up late.
- Never sleep longer than your husband or go back to bed after he leaves for work.
- Don't wear pretty clothes—that's prideful.

you do. I may write books and speak publicly, but there is no difference between us, except maybe that I'm older and have perhaps grown more tired of trying to prove how good I am.

I'm also telling you this because I hope to free you from the thought that God smiles on and uses only "good" people. If you've ever questioned that, take a look at Christ's words to Peter before Peter's denial: "When you have turned again, strengthen your brothers" (Luke 22:32). These words prove

- Don't look frumpy—you need to make sure your husband stays attracted to you.
- You must be attractive to your husband, but not so attractive that you appear vain or proud.
- You should have a gentle, quiet spirit . . . but being introverted is a sign of pride. ("I'm pretty much doomed either way!")
- You have cancer because of unresolved sin in your life.
- Serve in the church wherever there is a need, even if it means sacrificing your family life.
- You and your kids should always be dressed to the nines when you go to church.

THE *Good News*

The LORD has taken away the judgments against you;
he has cleared away your enemies.

ZEPHANIAH 3:15

that proud and spineless people like Peter (and you and me) can be used by the Lord to help others. We are not good, but He blesses us and uses us.

Oh, please be free from all the rules you think you need to obey to be used by the Lord! Be free from the rules this wicked world seeks to bind you with; be free from your own heart, which multiplies those rules without number. While it's true that God has worked in me and that He has been faithful to work transformation in me, I remain as dependent on His grace and mercy today as I was forty years ago—perhaps even more so.

"I've Got It Figured Out! Be like Me!"

It takes only a quick glance at a bookstore or at a lineup of popular speakers to realize how inundated we are with books and seminars with this message: "You can be great like me . . . if you follow my great advice (and buy my great book)." A friend recently told me that early in her faith, she attended a seminar where the speaker shared that his wife had read her Bible every single day of their marriage without fail and that her stellar Bible reading was the secret to their great marriage. My friend went home discouraged, wondering if this meant her marriage was doomed.

This is not the gospel message. It wasn't the message the Lord delivered, and it wasn't the message Paul preached. In fact, Paul counted all his religious accomplishments as "dung" (Philippians 3:8, KJV). Rather than boast about how good he was, he gave testimony to his failures in the Christian life: "I have the desire to do what is right, but not the ability to carry it out. For I do not do the good I want, but the evil I do not want is what I keep on doing" (Romans 7:18-19).

Aren't you thankful for his honesty here? Aren't you glad that he called himself the "foremost of sinners" (see 1 Timothy 1:15)? Aren't you grateful to hear the great apostle Paul say that his walk didn't always match his talk? I sure am! Think of it—the New Testament writers were nearly silent about their own success. They certainly didn't share "helpful tips for spiritual disciplines that I've already mastered." But they weren't silent about the good news that Jesus loves and welcomes sinners . . . and that is the one message we need to hear!

Have you never wondered why the Bible paints such a realistic (and bleak) picture of God's people of faith? Why paint these "heroes" from Scripture with such glaring honesty, with their faults exposed for all to see? Perhaps there's a message there for us: God loves to use sinners to accomplish His glorious goals. That way no one should be confused about who gets the glory. We are flawed human beings who serve a flawless God: "The saying is trustworthy and deserving of full acceptance, that Christ Jesus came into the world to save sinners" (1 Timothy 1:15).

"I Can Get Better—Really, I Can!"

Whenever we internalize the "helpful advice" of our Facebook friends, our Pinterest pals, the news nannies, or the latest "Christian" self-help books, or when we listen to our own legalistic hearts, there are only two possible outcomes: either we'll get angry with others who don't work as hard as we do or we'll give up in despair and sadness, thinking we'll never make the grade.

All these rules, no matter where they come from, are merely tools of our enemy to take our focus off Christ and put it on ourselves. The message of different or better rules is not what any of us need to hear, because rules cannot change our hearts. We need to hear the good news of a perfect Man who obeyed the only rule that mattered, the law of love, who swept away every superfluous "tip for a better life" and fulfilled the law perfectly in our place. He did so by loving His Father and us, His bride, flawlessly.

This is the Man who invited Himself for dinner at the home of a rich tax collector, to whom He spoke these glorious words: "The Son of Man came to seek and to save the lost" (Luke 19:10). He's the One Ezekiel prophesied about: "Behold, I, I myself will search for my sheep and will seek them out" (Ezekiel 34:11). He's the One who said, "I came not to call the righteous, but sinners" (Matthew 9:13). We don't need to hear more rules; we need to hear more good news about a Savior who loves sinners.

But here's the problem: even if you're nodding in agreement right now, even if you actually believe the good news about Jesus' perfectly keeping the law in your place, you still won't be convinced that it's enough—at least not when you can't seem to shed those dratted fifteen pounds, when your adopted kids have repaid your kindness with scorn, when your 401(k) just lost half its value, when you can't seem to keep your marriage together, or when your conscience just won't shut up about what a loser you are.

According to the director of one study, the self-improvement publishing market in the United States is worth an estimated $11.17 billion.[30] That's billions of dollars donated as an offering to our incurable faith in our perfectibility, our irrepressible faith in ourselves. The creed we confess with our lives is that if we just knew the right secrets, bought the right books, had the right mentors, or

I've gotten so many messages over the years about what God expects of me as "the perfect ministry wife." This doesn't come naturally for me, because I feel socially awkward, I'm not able to speak perfect wisdom to ladies, and I'm not necessarily part of the "in crowd." I'm also expected to open my home up to any woman who wants to come over, at any time, and be available to give whatever someone is asking from me. If someone is nitpicking me or criticizing me, I'm supposed to make myself vulnerable to that, as it's God's way of sanctifying me. It's seen as a sign of a lack of humility or an unrepentant heart to pull away from such relationships. It's easy for me to lose sight of the truth: that only Jesus is perfect, and the only way for me to be perfect is to embrace His perfection.

One Woman's
STORY

tried really, really, really hard this time, we'd be able to get our acts together.

If nothing else, this statistic should convince us that we're all believers in the power of "I can get better—really, I can!"

How many times have you started an exercise program or a new diet or a Bible-reading regimen or made a New Year's resolution, only to purpose to start doing better tomorrow or next Monday or next year? You can use all the little e-reminders you like, setting your phone to wake you up fifteen minutes early, already open to your Bible reading plan, and still turn it off and roll over.

Sure, you might be able to fulfill your commitment for a while, but what happens when it has been thirty-seven days since you've read and you're not sure you can stand to start and fail again? What happens when you've been reading consistently and you realize that you just reread the same passage you read yesterday but didn't even recognize it? What happens when you discover that a loved one has fallen behind in his commitment to read while you've persevered? What happens when you click on a link you know you shouldn't have clicked on or when you press Send on a message that you didn't mean to send and now it's too late to retrieve it? Who will save you when you're face-to-face with the undeniable truth that you still can't save yourself—that you're still the same old you?

There are only two possible destinations when you begin your race from a starting line that reads "I'm going to be better—really, I am." There will be either despair or pride, depression or anger, self-pity or contempt for others. There is no other possibility, because the race for self-perfection always turns us inward and therefore away from the only source of help—God's mercy and grace. The fires of hell at the end of that road are set ablaze with billions of self-help messages that whisper Satan's lie: "You will be like God" (Genesis 3:5). These messages teach us to trust in ourselves and our ability to get better, while they suffocate us in pride and despair and an ever-renewed, yet never-achieved, struggle toward freedom from failure.

"I Will Lay Down My Life for You"

We are all familiar with Peter's denial of Christ on the night of the Lord's betrayal. Peter's proud statement, "I will lay down my life for you" (John 13:37), could end in only one way: denial and despair. Peter's response after his denial is the inevitable epitaph on the headstone of every proud, self-trusting life: "He went out and wept bitterly" (Luke 22:62).[31]

Peter had a lesson he needed to learn—and it's the same one we need to learn too. It wasn't a lesson about how to believe in himself or how to stand strong against the winds of persecution or how to be a faithful friend or how to make a good confession. Peter needed to learn a lesson in humility and grace. Rather than boasting in his own strength, he needed to humbly throw himself on Christ's mercy. How many times have you gone out and wept bitterly in the face of your failures? What have those tears taught you? Have they taught you to try harder? I hope not.

We've all denied the Lord, just as Peter did. We've denied Him in both silly and significant conversations—with other little girls around the campfire and with the power brokers of this world. We've denied Him in our petty choices to turn away, and we've denied Him in our desire for a good reputation and self-protection. We know what it's like to feel crushed by guilt because we've blown it again. We resemble Peter more than we care to admit.

But there's another way we deny the Lord that might not occur to us: we deny Him when we long to feel good about ourselves for working hard to keep the rules. It doesn't matter how well intentioned those rules are. If we're trying to assure ourselves that we're okay and that God is happy with us because we've been good, in actuality *we're denying Christ*. Our pursuit of self-perfection is a denial of Christ because it is *His* work to make us okay, to justify us. And when we try to do it ourselves, we're basically saying that His work isn't enough; it isn't sufficient.

Not only that, but when we try to justify ourselves and garner self-approval by following all the rules, we're bound to fall into some sort of sin as a result. Here's an example to see how this might play out in our lives. If you think you have to make your house beautiful for Christmas so your family will have sweet memories and so you can go to bed at night feeling satisfied that you've done it all, you're bound to fall into either pride—looking down on the mom down the street who brought store-bought cookies to the neighborhood cookie exchange—or despair—feeling like a failure every time you go on Pinterest because you didn't have time to make egg-carton Nativity sets again today.

Both pride and despair breed other sins in their wake. If you think you've done it all and are congratulating yourself for having every stocking hung by the chimney with care, you'll be angry with your kids when they come tearing in and pull down the stockings trying to get to their goodies on Christmas morning. You'll also judge those who didn't get their mantel trimmings at half price last January during the after-Christmas sales. On the other hand, if the gift you're seeking is self-approval, then when you realize you've forgotten to order the kids' gifts on time, you'll start to berate yourself for all the times you've blown it in the past, and you'll decide you're a complete failure. You may even "go out and weep bitterly." There is failure here, but it has nothing to do with holiday planning. It's the failure to boast in your weaknesses.

It doesn't matter what law or rule or standard or step or hint we think we have to accomplish in order to approve of ourselves—we'll never achieve it. We'll never be perfect enough or consistent enough, and even if we somehow manage to achieve our goal, we'll realize once we get there that although we thought we had to take only three steps, we have another five to go.

When we buy into this law keeping, we play right into Satan's hands. He wants us to believe that God is too demanding and that we'll never be able to please Him, so we might as well just give up. Or he'd like to convince us that we're pretty good after all, so why would we need a Savior? When we try to find justification through keeping the law, we are essentially denying the life, death, resurrection, and ascension of Jesus—and that's really, really bad news.

Let Not Your Heart Be Troubled

How did Jesus respond to Peter, knowing Peter would inevitably fail Him, despite his proclamations of undying allegiance? Did Jesus lecture Peter or give him a pamphlet on becoming

THE *Ways We Beat* OURSELVES UP

What are some negative ways you respond to feelings of failure?

(The following responses were gathered from focus groups.)

- The messages start playing in my head: *I'm stupid. I'm not patient enough. I don't have any self-control.*
- I give up in despair, deciding it's too hard to figure out how to make it all work.
- Cry.
- Get angry.
- I resolve to try harder, telling myself, *I am going to fix this.*
- Get defensive.
- Become consumed with regret.
- Replay "what-ifs."
- Blame-shift.
- Put unfair expectations of perfection on myself for next time.
- Self-preach.
- Get down on myself.
- Feel ashamed.
- Sulk.
- Eat comfort food (especially chocolate).
- I feel hopeless, like there's no chance for change in me.
- I feel like all is lost, and I let my emotions take over and rule.
- I wallow.
- I get angry with myself for not having learned this lesson already. I want to hide my failure until I'm confident I will still be loved.

- I usually respond by mentally giving up—trying to keep peace at all costs.
- I often respond to feelings of failure by eating sweets, going to bed, or isolating myself.
- I look to momentary pick-me-ups (food, TV, social media, etc.).
- I harbor those feelings inside and replay them over and over again, refusing to accept God's forgiveness. I judge myself harshly and think I can't do anything right, especially things I should be good at.
- Feelings of failure send me into a crazy spiral of anxiety and fear, defeat and embarrassment, anger and shame. I think that failing is the absolute worst thing, and I can't ever recover from it.
- I respond with guilt and shame, wanting to cover up my failure somehow.
- I try to perform—to prove the accusation of failure wrong.
- I deal with feelings of failure by distraction (a learned message from culture), and by sadness (a message from my heart).
- I overthink areas of failure with the "would have, could have, should have" mentality.
- Try harder.

THE *Good News*

Let us then with confidence draw near to the throne of grace, that we may receive mercy and find grace to help in time of need. HEBREWS 4:16

a more masculine guy? Did He shame Peter for being such a weakling or tell him that he needed to believe in himself? No. Jesus cared for Peter's soul. He spoke the most comforting words of all to Peter and the rest of the disciples: "Let not your hearts be troubled" (John 14:1). Here is my paraphrase of Jesus' words to His self-assured disciples—and to us:

> During the most trying time of My life, you will fail Me. You are going to desert Me, deny Me, and betray Me. You say you are My friends, but I know you better than you know yourself. I know you are going to leave Me. Stop trying to prove your worthiness, and just believe. I know how you are going to sin against Me—that's why I'm here. So don't be troubled about how you will fail. Just believe. *Believe in God; believe also in Me.* I'm going to go and prepare a place for you where you will never fail again and where we will never be separated again. *I will come again and will take you to Myself, that where I am you may be also.* I love you so much I don't want to be without you. SEE JOHN 13:38–14:4

When Jesus said, "Let not your hearts be troubled," He was telling His disciples (and us, by extension) that they shouldn't be in distress. We shouldn't be "characterized by . . . distress or affliction or danger or need."[32] But we are, aren't we? Jesus had just told His disciples that He was leaving them and, what is more, that they would leave Him, too. So of course they were distressed. They were sure that if He would just give them clear directions on how to follow Him—if He would give them a road map to successful discipleship—they would be able to make it there.

But Jesus didn't give them a road map or a self-help book or even a pamphlet on how to follow Him—because He was going to a place where they couldn't go. In fact, He was going to atone for their sins. But He didn't shame them with their failure or guilt them into trying to be "manlier" or follow more rules. No, He told them that they need to believe.

Here's what He said:

> Believe in God; believe also in me. In my Father's house are many rooms. If it were not so, would I have told you that I go to prepare a place for you? And if I go and prepare a place for you, I will come again and will take you to myself, that where I am you may be also. . . . I am the way, and the truth, and the life. No one comes to the Father except through me. If you had known me, you would have known my Father also. From now on you do know him and have seen him.   JOHN 14:1-3, 6-7

The disciples needed to believe that Jesus wouldn't desert them, even though they were about to desert Him. They needed to believe that His eternal mission was to bring His sinful people to live with Him in complete bliss forever. They needed to believe that Jesus was building a home for their souls—and that this construction project was in His competent hands. They needed to believe that He was going to do all the work that was necessary to bring a smile to the Father's face.

We're just like the disciples, aren't we? We are proud, confused, boastful weaklings. We think that the Lord will desert us for our failures. But we're wrong. Jesus never tells us the seventeen things we need to do to be better people. He simply tells us to believe in Him.

Nothing More to Add

Jesus is the *way* to the Father. He is "both the sacrifice for our sins and the Mediator of the new covenant."[33] He is the way to all we need, so we must not be troubled. He is the way to a relationship with God—a way to acceptance and welcome from Him. He is the way to freedom from despair and pride. "If it were not so, would I have told you that I go to prepare a place for you?" (John 14:2). Believe that He is not lying when He says that He's all you need. "Let not your hearts be troubled" (John 14:1).

He is the *truth*. This means that He is "the Word made flesh, the final word God has spoken to his people."[34] There aren't any more words that we need to hear about how to please God. Jesus has done it all. If you want to know God's disposition toward you, look to Jesus and what He has done. "From now on you do know him [the Father] and have seen him" (John 14:7). That's His promise, that's His work, that's what He has already done. There's nothing more you need to add. When you hear about Jesus' love for you, you can know that He is representing the Father's love for you as well.

He is the *life*. He is the "life from the sovereign giver of life, the eternal Father—who gives life now and in the coming age for eternity."[35] If you believe, you have His life now and for eternity. But when we fail to believe—when we reject that He is all we need and that He has already done it all—we are really denying Him. But even then, even when we falter and doubt and think we just need the right self-help book (again!), He still loves us and welcomes us and provides for us. We no longer need to be afraid that He's going to shut us out because of our failures. He knows them all, and yet He keeps on loving us. He's got it all; He's done it all.

Freedom from Troubled Hearts

We all have troubled hearts, because we have all been told that there are millions of things we must do in order to make God pleased with us. (And we've bought it!) This kind of thinking always ends up making us proud, angry, and judgmental— or despairing, fearful, and unbelieving. The only way to be free from this heart trouble is to believe. We can believe that God is as good and powerful and wise and loving as He says He is . . . and then we can rest. We can accept His peace so our hearts don't have to be troubled or afraid. We can have complete rest, knowing that He has done everything that ever needed to be done for us (see John 14:27).

Theologian C. F. W. Walther said, "The Gospel does not require anything good that man must furnish: not a good heart, not a good disposition, no improvement of his condition, no godliness, no love either of God or men. . . . It plants love into his heart and makes him capable of all good works. It demands nothing, but it gives all. Should not this fact make us leap for joy?"[36] Think of that: the gospel doesn't require anything from us, and it gives everything to us. That means we can finally rest and cease our continual striving for self-approval. The Lord loves us as we are now . . . not as we might be at some point in the future. So we can relax into His capable hands.

Questions FOR REFLECTION AND DISCUSSION

1. Did my confession of my sin of pride at the beginning of the chapter discourage or encourage you? Why?

2. Can you think of any reasons why Christians should be the most transparent sinners in the world? What stops us from being transparent?

3. What do you think it means to boast in your weakness? Is this something you've done before? If so, what happened? If not, why not?

4. Which do you struggle with more: despair or pride? What does this struggle look like for you?

5. What did Jesus mean when He told His disciples to have trouble-free hearts? Does this describe you? Why or why not?

6. Summarize what you've learned in this chapter in four or five sentences.

CHAPTER 6

WHO IS YOUR GOD?

When I was at my hair salon recently, a woman there told me with some regret that she was falling behind in her New Year's resolution. She had committed to cleaning out a room every day, but ten days into the year, she was already failing.

"But," she said, "I'll make up for it this year by getting trained to be a hot yoga instructor."

So while she felt guilty because she wasn't cleaning her house the way she wanted to, she was still making progress in another area. I doubt that pleasing God ever crossed her mind. Rather, like most people in our secularized culture, she was hoping to earn her own self-benediction.

Most of us just want to look in the mirror and feel good

about ourselves. We are chasing an ever-elusive dream: we want to believe we are good enough. The way we live has more to do with our own opinions, our own rules, and our own self-approval than with what any deity might declare from on high. As a society, we view the fear of God as the trapping of an ignorant past, when Neanderthals thought a solar eclipse necessitated the sacrifice of a chicken or a virgin or a virgin chicken. In general, our society doesn't care much about trying to merit God's favor—in fact, many of us rarely think about His favor at all.

"Let's Talk about Me!"

For Christians, though, it should be a different story. And it is—at least in part. I think most Christians sincerely do want to please God, and yet somehow we've failed to make the connection between the work of Jesus Christ and our own work. In far too many churches, the wonderful truths of the gospel have not been clearly taught, so we are unaware of the great riches that are already ours. Most of us know that our sins have been forgiven because of Jesus' death on Calvary, but we've never thought deeply about what His sinless life and bodily resurrection might mean when we're faced with our failures.

When we go to church, instead of hearing the good news that our sins have been forgiven (absolution) and that righteousness has already been granted to us (justification), we often hear about the three or five or thirty-five steps we need to take in order to earn some blessing from God. We acknowledge our shortcomings, but all too often the proposed answer is self-salvation projects. The good news that God's smile (benediction) already rests on us hardly, if ever, crosses our minds. We forget that we are one with His beloved Son and therefore are *already* loved and counted perfect.

The Puritan pastor Walter Marshall wrote that most Christians fall into this "key error": "They think that even though they have been justified by a righteousness produced solely by Christ, they are sanctified [changed, transformed] by a holiness produced solely by themselves."[37]

We do not earn God's smile by our own works after we are saved any more than we did before we were saved. But although we might give tacit agreement to this truth, we still think that there's something more we need to do in order to make God happy and earn blessings from Him.

Ignorance of the good news is not our only problem. In fact, I don't think it's our primary one. Sure, some of us may not be able to define justification, but even among those who can, there's a deeper disconnect in our hearts. We hear about forgiveness and justification and have to stifle a yawn. We're apathetic; we're bored with all this God talk. The cry of our hearts, whether we actually verbalize it or not, is this: *Justification, schmustification! Let's talk about me! Sure, Jesus may have done the work of making me right with God, but what about me? I just want to be free from all this guilt!*

We're like Bette Midler's character in the 1988 movie *Beaches*, who said, "But enough about me, let's talk about you. What do *you* think of me?"[38] We may not be so blatant about it, but that's pretty much how the priorities stack up in the quiet places of our hearts. Despite the fact that we're loved and welcomed by our heavenly Father, we want to look at our lives and feel satisfied that we've earned our own approval; we want to feel good about ourselves, to be free from guilt.

Our principal concern is not that we don't have God's approval; it's that we don't really care that we do. Need proof? Have you ever thought, *I know that God forgives me, but I just can't forgive myself*? Aside from the fact that self-forgiveness isn't even hinted at in Scripture, this impulse to seek okay-ness in our own eyes is a clear indication of our apathy about God's opinion and our bondage to our own. For the majority of Christians, the most pressing question is not, How can I be right with God? but rather, How can I be right in my own eyes?

So perhaps the real question all of us need to ask is this: Who is our god? Are we worshiping the one true God, or are we worshiping ourselves?

We foolishly believe that God is something of a pushover—that because He's God, He's obligated to be nice to us and forgive us. That's His job, after all! So we nod at His gracious approval and continue to demand our own. We believe He has forgiven us, and we think that's great and all. But His opinion isn't the one that really matters—at least not at three o'clock in the morning when we're trying to shut out the incessant harassment of our inner slave driver.

We think we want to hear a message about ourselves from ourselves—a message that will assure our hearts—and yet no message of self-benediction ("Your good really does outweigh your bad!") or self-absolution ("I forgive myself—anybody in my shoes would have done the same!") is ever loud enough to drown out that damning voice. And no self-inspired message is convincing enough to make us believe it's true.

"If Jesus Is So Great, Why Am I Not Happy?"

When we are driven by self-forgiveness, self-approval, and self-perfection, our faith will inevitably be poisoned by misery and guilt. We make lousy gods, and our quest to find okay-ness in our own eyes will always lead to difficulties in our relationships and unrest in our souls. We will never know peace or joy. We will find it impossible to love.

Given the conflicting messages we receive about what it takes to be "good enough," it's not surprising that Christians are as plagued by depression and anxiety as the general population is and that we are just as likely to take psychotropic drugs.[39] It is impossible to mix faith in God with faith in our own perfectibility and not have some sort of blowup or breakdown somewhere. As Christians, we've been wrongly taught that having God in our lives automatically makes us better people. But at the same time we're taught that a victorious life is within our grasp, if only we follow the "secret steps." Then when we struggle with failure, we assume that there must be something wrong with us—something that isn't wrong with everyone else. We become distressed when we can't keep the rules of good behavior that have been dangled before us by other "successful" Christian women who seem to have successfully climbed Mount Perfection and planted their "I'm really great!" flags for all to see.

We're also suffering because we're being crushed by

Bad Advice WOMEN RECEIVE

What are the dumbest things people tell women they have to do in order to be godly?

(These are real responses from my recent Facebook post.)

- Your child's disability is a result of your lack of faith or your lack of prayer.
- If you are single and lonely, then you're not making Jesus your "all in all."
- If you have a fussy baby, it's either because you're spoiling the child or because you're being punished for past sin.
- If you want to have a baby but are unable to get pregnant, you need to trust the Lord more.
- Be content!
- Godliness is living in the country, growing your own food, and having a large family.
- Never say no to sex with your husband.

unexpected guilt—the guilt that comes with the knowledge of ongoing failure. The more we buy into this "self-perfection through quasi-Christian rule-keeping" mentality, the more depressed and anxious we'll be.

That's because true transformation can never come from within—no matter how hard we try. Whether we go the way of traditionalism, living like the Amish in a little house on the prairie, or the way of liberalism, getting tatted up and donning combat boots, we still won't be able to approve of

- You must always be joyful as a mother/wife/woman.
- If you suffer from anxiety or depression, it's because you are embracing sin and you aren't trusting God.
- Do everything with "excellence"—which translates to perfection.
- If you are a pastor's wife, you must play the piano, lead women's Bible studies, and be at every church function.
- Do your best, and God will do the rest.
- Never get a tattoo, even a meaningful one. Tattoos are evil and unbiblical.
- Don't talk about your sin, or you'll give Jesus a bad name.
- Never question God.

THE Good News

[The Lord says,] "I will satisfy the weary soul, and every languishing soul I will replenish." JEREMIAH 31:25

ourselves, because our own works are too weak and flawed to transform our consciences.

"But I Thought I Was Going to Be Different!"

When I was a young girl, I remember praying to some god I didn't really know that I wouldn't be the same failure tomorrow that I had been that day. Then I'd get up the next day and hit "replay," only to do it all over again.

During my teen years, I ran headlong into a life of drugs, sex, and rock and roll, seeking in vain to silence my conscience. I lived a life that was debauched in every possible way available to a woman in the 1970s.

By the time I hit my late teens and early twenties, I had pretty much given up thinking I would ever be anything other than a degenerate loser, so I tried to anesthetize my conscience with partying and by telling myself I was okay because some dude liked me.

Then, in astonishing grace and out of lavish mercy, Christ saved me. I'll never forget the wonderful relief from guilt I experienced in that moment. There really was a God, and He loved me!

But it didn't take long for my old companion guilt to assault me again, and I didn't know how to fight it. Yes, I belonged to Jesus. Yes, I believed He had died for me. But I was still sinful. And to my surprise, I was also still weak. I didn't hear all the wonderful truths of the good news, or if I did, I thought they were for those unbelievers in the back row.

Before long, the chains of guilt that had been loosed when I was saved were soon binding my soul again. So I tried harder and rededicated my life over and over again. I looked incessantly for the secret to freedom from sin and guilt. I prayed the right prayers, and I read the Bible incessantly. I thought that if I married into a respectable family, I would be okay. So I pursued Phil. I thought that if I had children and kept them from sinning like I had, I would be okay. So I hammered my kids with the law every day.

All of this was a result of my desire to be freed from my

sin, free from my guilt. I wanted to be able to look at myself in the mirror and know that I was okay. But I never could—not on my own, anyway.

Bowing before the Throne of Rules

We may not realize it, but our desire for self-forgiveness, self-acceptance, and self-perfection is actually a form of idolatry in our lives. We think that our opinion and our own successes are of highest importance. We worship our own judgments and in doing so, degrade God's.

The idolatry of self-worship is nothing new. In some ways we're like the Judaizers in the early church, who tried to get the people in Galatia to add rules to the grace they'd already been given. They were wrongly teaching the people that they needed to add circumcision and food laws to their Christianity.

Sound familiar? Like these early Christians, we give lip service to the fact that we have God's approval through the work of Christ, but we think we need to add something to it—just to be sure. We want to get to the end of the day and assuage our consciences that the guilt we're feeling is undeserved. We want to smile on ourselves.

This is not Christianity. Paul wrote strong words of correction to the Galatians warning against this mixing of grace and human works: "I am astonished that you are so quickly deserting him who called you in the grace of Christ and are turning to a different gospel. . . . For am I now seeking the approval of man, or of God? Or am I trying to please man?

If I were still trying to please man, I would not be a servant of Christ" (Galatians 1:6, 10).

Paul was "astonished" that the Galatians were so quickly deserting the message of grace. The word *astonished* here actually means that Paul was "extraordinarily disturbed" by their desertion of the Lord and His gracious good news.[40] We should be too.

Paul knew how this desertion would play out in their lives. He knew it's impossible for anyone to live for self-approval, in bondage to his or her conscience, while at the same time serving Christ. Paul goes on to make a clear statement about our okay-ness: if it were possible to be made right with God through rule keeping, then "Christ died for no purpose" (Galatians 2:21). Paul was so astonished by the Galatians' turning from the message of grace that he actually wondered what witch had cast a spell on them (see Galatians 3:1). Why would they think that earning their own merit before God (and each other) would be better than receiving it as a gracious gift? Why do we think it? It's insanity.

The good news is that Christians are no longer under the law. God's blessings are not dependent on whether we obey the rules. We have been redeemed from the curse of death. We are no longer slaves in God's house, hoping to earn His favor or secure our place there. No, we are dearly loved as adopted sons. Sonship means that every right, privilege, and inheritance that was to be given to the firstborn male of the house is now available to us (whether female or male).

Think about it—if Paul saw the list of things we think we have to do today in order to make God happy with us, he would likely pull out his hair and call us bewitched fools too. He would wonder who had deceived us into thinking Jesus isn't enough. Why would we place ourselves under such bondage when we've been given complete freedom? Why would we "submit again to a yoke of slavery" (Galatians 5:1)? Why would we listen to the voice of guilt when forgiveness has been freely granted to us?

Believing He's Not Enough

Our worship of the rules is not our only problem; we also get tripped up by our unbelief. We don't believe that God's approval is sufficient for us. We think we have His forgiveness, but that's not very satisfying. We want to forgive ourselves. I've actually heard people say, "I want to change so I don't have to keep asking for forgiveness." We seem to have forgotten that weakness was the very thing Paul boasted in. The bottom line is that we don't believe Jesus' perfection is enough for us. We accept that He loves us, but we want to be loved by ourselves even more. We don't believe that His love is enough to satisfy our hearts. We want something concrete, something tangible.

These are all problems of faith. We've never entered into the rest that has been promised to us through faith in Christ. We're still wandering around the wilderness, trying to be strong enough to win all our battles on our own. Sure, if God wants to pitch in to help us out a bit, that's great, but ultimately it's up to us to do our best. After all, "God helps those who help themselves," right?[41] We are ignoring the warnings

from the book of Hebrews—warnings against going back to
the rules, seeking our okay-ness from ourselves, and leaning
on our techniques of self-perfection and self-deception.

> Who were those who heard and yet rebelled? Was it
> not all those who left Egypt led by Moses? And with
> whom was he provoked for forty years? Was it not
> with those who sinned, whose bodies fell in the wil-
> derness? And to whom did he swear that they would
> not enter his rest, but to those who were disobedi-
> ent? So we see that they were unable to enter because
> of unbelief. HEBREWS 3:16-19

An entire generation of Israelites—those whose bodies
fell in the wilderness—failed to believe that God was as good
and loving as He said He was and that His love was all they
needed. They fell because they didn't believe He really loved
them and would take care of them and bring them into a
land that flowed with milk and honey. They knew they didn't
deserve His blessing, and they assumed He was faithless and
demanding like they were. They thought He would treat
them the way they deserved to be treated. And so they wandered and wandered and never found rest until their corpses
were laid in the desert.

There is good news: a promised rest awaits all who believe.
But we may fail to experience it, especially if our hearts are
agitated by our own rules and our failure to obey them. Rest
comes to those who trust and believe that Jesus was perfect
on our behalf—that He obeyed all the rules in our place, as
our representative.

In college I started really paying attention to what kind of woman God wanted me to be. At the time, I was planning to marry a boy from a small, cult-like church that required women to be quiet and submissive. The only acceptable role for women was to be perfect home-schooling homemakers. I had been raised in a controlling environment, so this seemed like a perfect plan. Later the church decided I was not a good match for this young man, but it took years for me to let go of this message about relationships and what it meant to be a "good girl." I'm so grateful to have experienced the true gospel—that we are saved through what Christ has done, not through anything we can do.

One Woman's
—◦❧ STORY ❧◦—

Why is it so hard for us to believe and enter into rest? Many times it's because believing in Him means not believing in ourselves. We must give up false confidence in ourselves to embrace the humiliation of the Cross. God is asking us to believe that His perfection is enough for us. And then to believe it over and over again, every day, until we finally stop hoping for our own approval and rest.

Failure to believe always results in our restlessness and

thrashing about, trying to find a way to become better. But we don't need to live like this—He has something so much better in mind. Jesus' command to His disciples was a command to believe in Him (see John 6:29). Our necessary act of obedience is simply to believe that He is taking care of us and that what He has already done for us is indeed all that needs to be done.

A Promise and a Death

Our tendency to bow down before rules and doubt God's perfection on our behalf is nothing new. We first began to notice ourselves and judge our okay-ness in the Garden of Eden. Before Adam and Eve fell, they didn't feel a need to cover their nakedness. They had nothing to hide. They weren't ashamed; they had never experienced guilt (see Genesis 2:25). It never would have occurred to them that they needed anything more than what God had already given them. They were blind to themselves but saw each other and their Lord perfectly.

But then they chose to sin, and "the eyes of both were opened, and they knew that they were naked. And they sewed fig leaves together and made themselves loincloths" (Genesis 3:7).

Oh, cursed knowledge of good and evil! Cursed dissatisfaction and guilt! Cursed unbelief!

As women who have lived with the awareness of our own shame, failure, guilt, and sin our entire lives, we simply can't imagine what it would be like to live a life free from consciousness of our own nakedness. What a terrible turn we took that fateful day! Seeking to be more like God, we became slaves—always seeking and never finding self-forgetfulness.

If there were one object that represented the entire history of humanity since the Fall, it would have to be a mirror. After that point, we stopped looking outward and upward. Now we spend all our time looking down and within. But thanks be to God—our story doesn't end there!

Right on the heels of the Fall, God made a promise to His shamed children. Then He covered them. This was His promise: a Conqueror would come who would crush the head of our enemy (see Genesis 3:15). The enemy—the one who had so hatefully questioned whether God's goodness and love were enough—would not have the final say. He would not be victorious. No, a Deliverer would come into the world, and He would come through the offspring of the woman. Eve, the deceived one who brought destruction to us all, would not bear her shame and nakedness forever. Instead, she would be the vehicle the Lord would use to reassure women (and men) everywhere that He loves us and that all we need to do is believe His promise and trust in His promised One.

God loves to use flawed women (just like Eve, just like me, just like you) to bring His blessings to the world. And so He sent His beloved Son to be humiliated and shamed for us. He sent Him to bear the guilt of our sin. He sent Him to hang in nakedness and be deserted by all—even His Father—for us.

After God made His promise to Adam and Eve, He sealed

it in blood. A poor animal, which had never before known fear of man, cried out in terror as it was slaughtered and skinned to provide a covering for them (see Genesis 3:21).

After their fall, Adam and Eve needed to be able to look at themselves and see something besides their own inadequacies. So they were given the flesh and blood of an innocent animal. They were no longer ashamed because of their nakedness, but that didn't solve their deeper problem.

Now they were ashamed because of their sin, and no mere animal would ever be able to obliterate their inner nakedness— the shame and guilt they felt. That shame had to be cleansed through the blood of Eve's promised Son. Innocent human blood would have to be shed for human sin. There would be no cleansing of conscience, no freedom from guilt and shame, until the spotless Lamb cried out in terror on that other tree. There would be no absolution or benediction until His side poured out that cleansing blood and water.

The book of Hebrews says, "If the blood of goats and bulls . . . [will] sanctify for the purification of the flesh, how much more will the blood of Christ, who through the eternal Spirit offered himself without blemish to God, *purify our conscience* from dead works to serve the living God" (Hebrews 9:13-14, emphasis added).

The dead works spoken of here are all those things we do to try to approve of ourselves and to earn God's approval— to clean ourselves up. The only way out of this slavery to dead works is to know that our consciences have already been purified and that we are without blemish before Him. If we don't take the good news of the gospel as the only antidote to our weaknesses, sin, and slavery to self-approval—if the grace of God doesn't flood and satiate our souls—then stupid rules about how to make ourselves better will take over. Something must occupy the center of our lives, and if it isn't the strong medicine of the good news, it will be the poison of stupid rules.

Hebrews 10:14 says, "By a single offering [Jesus] has *perfected for all time* those who are being sanctified" (emphasis added). In other words, Jesus has set us free from our preoccupation with ourselves so we can rest in Him alone. We can put our mirrors away—we don't need them anymore. We have been "perfected for all time."

Questions FOR REFLECTION AND DISCUSSION

1. According to the Bible, we can "have confidence to enter the holy places by the blood of Jesus" so that we can "draw near with a true heart in full assurance of faith" (Hebrews 10:19, 22). Would you say that your relationship with the Lord is marked by confidence before Him? Do you have full assurance in your faith? Why or why not?

2. Paul chided the Galatians about adding rules to grace in an attempt to please God. Why was Paul so upset by this? In what ways have you tried to do something similar?

3. Read 1 John 2:15-16. Have you ever considered that your desire for self-approval is a form of worldliness?

How do you think the "desires of the eyes" and the "pride of life" might be tied to self-approval?

4. At the end of the day, when your head hits the pillow, do you care that God is pleased with you—simply because of what Christ has done on your behalf? Read Romans 12:2. What do you think it means to be "transformed by the renewal of your mind"?

5. Read Hebrews 9:13-14. What do you think this passage means when it says that our consciences have been purified? Do you believe you've been "perfected for all time" (Hebrews 10:14)? How would this knowledge change the way you view yourself and the rules you come up against?

6. Summarize what you've learned in this chapter in four or five sentences.

CHAPTER 7

HE SAID *US!*

THE YEAR 2012 was a difficult one for my husband, Phil, and me. Phil was laid off from the job he'd had for more than thirty years in a company he had actually owned at one time, and as a result, we had to find less expensive housing in rural San Diego. After moving away from the place we'd called home for a decade and from the neighbors and community we'd established there, I felt isolated, hopeless, and alone. During this time Phil was also experiencing health difficulties, and we were in the process of changing churches. Then, in a surprising turn of events, he was rehired by the same company. We were extremely grateful, but now he had a long commute to work. Honestly, I just didn't understand what God was up to. We'd been praying for wisdom and guidance, but the road seemed bumpy and unclear.

Then, in the midst of all this, Phil's dear mother, Thelma, began to show increasing signs of dementia that made her fearful and occasionally violent. This was particularly hard for me to bear, because Thelma had been a truly godly woman. She had attended a Bible college and had faithfully served Christ as a young woman, preaching the gospel in the hills of Ohio, Kentucky, and West Virginia.

I first met Thelma when she was in her early fifties and teaching mission classes at our church's Bible college. She took extended trips to Japan, Mexico, and South America, bringing the gospel message to those who had never heard it. After her children were grown, she and her husband moved into a trailer in southern Texas so she could attend language school for two years in preparation for mission work in Tijuana.

Thelma was an integral part of every church she attended. She built libraries, shared her testimony, taught Sunday school, vacuumed the sanctuary, and played the piano for worship services. She also practiced hospitality like no one I've ever met. Someone was always coming to stay with Mom and Dad, and she'd happily treat them to chicken and dumplings or apple slices. It was from her that I learned I could eat gravy for breakfast and make fudge for dessert. My grandchildren, her great-grandchildren, called her "Candy Grandma." I'll let you guess why.

I say all this by way of background because I want you to understand the confusion and doubt I felt while I watched her slip away. I know that all people, even those we call saints, die at some point. I understand that death can be a long process, for Christians and non-Christians alike. What I didn't understand was why God would allow someone who had devoted her life to Him to suffer so much terror during her last few months. Why didn't the Lord just take her?

I was scrambling to find answers. I needed something from the Lord that would help me understand—something that would take the edge off the confusion and the pain. Day after day, I asked, "Why, God?" I prayed. I cried. I was a mess.

And I have a hunch I'm not alone. At some point in our lives, we all face circumstances that leave us confused and hopeless. We are all plagued by guilt, and we know we're not cutting it, but we pigheadedly keep searching for a secret key that will enable us to live the lives we think we want to live, which only produces more guilt. We're hoping for a change that will empower us to look in the mirror and approve of ourselves—or at least rest in peace when the end finally comes. We're hoping someone will tell us the secret about how to gain God's approval, so we pile rule after rule upon ourselves.

We wrongly think that if we could just discover the right steps to take, every troubling circumstance would either disappear or at least begin to make more sense than it does right now. Sometimes we think that if we just had strong enough faith or deep enough wisdom, all the situations that trouble us would fade away.

I keep thinking that somehow I might be able to do all that God—or my own conscience masquerading as God— demands of me. Sometimes I wish God would make an appearance and clean me up—and everyone else, too. I wish He'd come down from heaven and help us all out of the messes we're in. I wish He'd tell me why He does what He does—why He allows the righteous to suffer. Sometimes I think that the reason I don't understand His ways is because my faith isn't strong enough or because I haven't discovered the key that would unlock all His secrets.

"Lord, where are You in this mess?" It's a question I've asked in the past, and one I continue to ask.

If Scripture is any indication, I'm not the first person who has had such a longing.

About seven hundred years before the birth of Jesus, the prophet Isaiah prayed a similar prayer. Like us, Isaiah lived during a time when God's people were craving worldly security. According to the *ESV Study Bible*, the question forced upon the Israelites was one of trust: "In what will God's people trust for salvation—in human strategies of self-rescue, or in prophetic promises of divine grace?"[42]

Isaiah prayed, "Oh that you would rend the heavens and come down . . . to make your name known to your adversaries, and that the nations might tremble at your presence! . . . From of old no one has heard or perceived by the ear, no eye has seen a God besides you, who acts for those who wait for him" (Isaiah 64:1-2, 4).

Can you hear the heart of God's prophet? Yes, he was heartbroken, but at the same time, he was hopeful. He knew that it would take something absolutely earth shattering for God to clean up the mess made by humanity, but he also knew that God can do the unimaginable. Isaiah knew that nothing he could do—no works of his hands—would ever be enough. He hoped that God would act for those who simply waited for Him. Isaiah was longing for a cataclysmic event. It would take a tearing-open of the sky, a great condescension from heaven to earth. And shockingly, that's exactly what the Lord did! Some seven hundred years after Isaiah's prophecies, the Lord rent the heavens and sent His Son—God incarnate—to the world.

When Self-Scrubbing Isn't Enough

At the beginning of His public ministry, Jesus sought out His cousin John, who was baptizing in the Jordan River. When Jesus asked to be baptized, John's response was the right one: "I need to be baptized by you, and do you come to me?" (Matthew 3:14). Even John, the last and greatest prophet under the old covenant (see Matthew 11:11), knew he wasn't good enough. Like us, he was plagued by an awareness of his own guilt. And like us, he struggled with unbelief (see Matthew 11:3).

John knew he was a sinner, and he needed someone to cleanse him—someone who could make him righteous. Jesus knew this too. John needed a righteousness far beyond what he could accomplish on his own. No matter how strict he was with himself, no matter how much he denied himself the pleasures of the world and lived as an ascetic in the wilderness, it would never be enough. That's because outward righteousness can never satisfy the demands of a holy God, who not only hears our words and sees our deeds but also judges the thoughts and intentions of our hearts (see Hebrews 4:12-13).

John knew his own heart, and he knew that even though he was preaching repentance, he would never be able to repent enough to be right with God.

The righteousness John needed was a righteousness that had to come from outside himself—a righteousness that Jesus was accomplishing at that very moment. This righteousness was the perfect obedience to the law—inward and outward. Here was Jesus' response to John: "Let it be so now; it is proper for us to do this to fulfill all righteousness" (Matthew 3:15, NIV). Did you catch that? The holy Son of God joined Himself in union with sinful John and said, "It is proper for *us* to do this to fulfill all righteousness" (emphasis added).

Just what was Jesus doing there in those muddy waters, submitting Himself to a baptism for sinners? He walked into that muddy water because that is where we are, trying to clean ourselves up. He knew we needed someone so pure that His purity couldn't be defiled by muddy water. Only someone as holy as Jesus could make dirty women and men clean.

And so, down He went. And John understood, as much as he could, that it was right for this righteous Man to go into the muddy water with him. We know that we, too, need someone who will be righteous for us in all our religious rites, in our baptism, in our persistent self-scrubbing.

Generations before, Joshua and the Levites had brought the Ark of the Covenant, the dwelling place of God's very presence, into the water of the Jordan so the people could cross over into the Promised Land (see Joshua 3). In much the same way, Jesus, the God-Man, brought the very presence of God back into the Jordan to assure us of our safe arrival in the land of rest He has promised us. But unlike that earlier day, when the people were warned to keep their distance from the Ark, Jesus invited John's touch. He called him—and us—to come near Him. Jesus, our Brother, is standing in that water with us.

Scripture tells us that as Jesus walked into the water, He was praying (see Luke 3:21). Perhaps He was praying for us; perhaps He was confessing our sins. We don't know, but we do know He was standing with us, in our place, completely identifying with us. In doing so, He transformed all baptismal water from an ordinary natural element into a soul-cleansing shower that signifies life and righteousness in the heart of the believer. Only Jesus can turn ordinary water into water that can wash a soul.

Entering Our Muck

At last, Isaiah's prayer that God's presence would invade our mud and muck was answered. Immediately after Jesus came up from the water, the "heavens were opened to him" (Matthew 3:16). God's longed-for presence was finally invading this wicked world, and the sins we could never cleanse were washed white as snow (see Isaiah 1:18). God had opened the door to the Promised Land, and after hundreds of years of sin, failure, self-reliance, and guilt on the part of God's people, those prayers for God's cleansing presence were being fulfilled.

How did God answer Isaiah's prayer to make His name known to His adversaries (see Isaiah 64:1-2)? He tore open

Bad Advice WOMEN RECEIVE

What are the dumbest things people tell women they have to do in order to be godly?

(These are real responses to the question I posted on Facebook.)

- To be a godly woman, you must be creative, crafty, artistic, and able to make your home fit the culturally accepted standard of beautiful—and you must do it on a tiny budget. It helps if you scrapbook and can make almost anything out of pretty paper.
- Submit without question to church authority, especially if you're a single woman. It's not appropriate to share a different viewpoint or express disagreement.
- Discipline your children all day to make sure your house is peaceful and orderly when your husband gets home. After all, he has worked so hard all day—he deserves this!
- Be organized, know everything that's going on, have a perfect house, make homemade meals every night,

the heavens and came down, but not in anger and judgment, in fire and condemnation, as we deserve. No, He came down in peace, in the form of a dove, and rested on Jesus. Then the voice from heaven pronounced the most beautiful benediction ever heard: "You are my beloved Son; with you I am well pleased" (Luke 3:22).

bake, sew, clean, and be a great budgeter. Basically be the perfect homemaker.

- Clip coupons.
- Don't use birth control. Allow God to choose the size of your family.
- Always wear that "ministry smile."
- Don't pursue any activities you might enjoy that do not involve your children or your husband.
- If you're single and struggling with loneliness, you should be okay with being "married to Jesus."
- As a wife, you are to orient your life around your husband. You no longer have your own identity; you are only an extension of your husband.
- Check your brain and heart at the door, but bring your body to cook, clean, have sex, and give birth to babies.

THE *Good News*

I have been crucified with Christ. It is no longer I who live, but Christ who lives in me . . . for if righteousness were through the law, then Christ died for no purpose. GALATIANS 2:20-21

The Spirit of God entered the Son of Man, and from that moment on, all who believe in God's Son receive that same benediction: "You are my beloved son [or daughter]; with you I am well pleased." Why? How can that be? Because He has washed us. We are clean. We are one with Him by the Spirit. And in that moment, all who are given the gift of faith—all who trust in this wet, muddy Man standing in this insignificant river—have the same benediction. We are His beloved children. He is pleased with us.

Is that hard for you to believe? Of course it is—but it is the truth. He is pleased with you whether you did your devotions this morning or not. He is pleased with you on the days you get up determined to love Him and on the days you roll out of bed thirty minutes late and can't remember His name. He is pleased with you whether you fall into that same stupid sin again or whether, by His grace, you shun it. He is pleased with you because He is pleased with His Son, and His Son said that blessed word *us* in reference to you: "It is fitting for *us* to fulfill all righteousness" (Matthew 3:15). Jesus has done it all for us . . . and with us.

Into the Wilderness

Jesus left the water that marked Him as God's chosen One to enter forty days of temptation in the wilderness. This forty-day period is a nod to Israel's forty-year temptation in the wilderness (see Numbers 14:33). But unlike Israel, Jesus did not succumb to the devil.

Jesus was a real human—a flesh-and-blood Being who needed to eat and sleep just as we do. And Jesus faced Satan's temptation when He was physically at His weakest. Matthew tells us that "after fasting forty days and forty nights, [Jesus] was hungry" (Matthew 4:2). Why would Matthew make such an obvious statement? Because he wanted us to know that Jesus wasn't some superhero who didn't need food. Yes,

He was and is God, but He never allowed Himself the privilege of accessing His deity to make life easier for Himself. He didn't use any superpowers to fight the devil. He fought as a human being, as one of us.

Jesus had been without food and a good night's sleep for well over a month. He was painfully hungry and tired, yet He fought on. I shudder to think of all the times I've been irritable and hopeless because I didn't get a good night's sleep. On those days I rationalize that I'm "just exhausted" or "simply starving" when I respond unkindly, grumble under my breath, or check out of life and do whatever I want to do.

How many times have we snapped at someone because we were hungry? How many times have we been irritable because we didn't get enough sleep? How many times have we said, "I know I'm cranky, but I'm PMS-ing"? We need someone who will be righteous for us in our weakness, someone who will be with us in our most desperate frailties. That's why God opened the heavens and came down to walk as one of us. He walks with us in weakness, pain, suffering, and sorrow—and ultimately in victory.

Our Enemy's Arsenal

What was Satan's first effort to tempt the Lord? It was the same one he used to tempt Adam and Eve in the Garden and Israel in the wilderness. Satan tempted them with food, as he did to Jesus: "The tempter came and said to [Jesus], 'If you are the Son of God, command these stones to become loaves of bread'" (Matthew 4:3). But although food is significant, it's not the real issue here. The critical point is whether we believe that God's Word for us, about us, and to us is sufficient for us. Do we believe it's enough to be called His beloved daughter or son? Or will we try to make bread out of those lifeless stones we find in our own lives? When we face disappointment, discouragement, and questions that seem to have no answer, will His Word suffice for us, or will we demand something more?

At any point, the One who later identified Himself as the Manna, the Bread of Life (see John 6:35-59), could have fed Himself. On two separate occasions He made bread to feed the hungry (see Matthew 14:13-21; 15:32-39). But He wasn't about to fall into the old trap that Eve had fallen into. She wanted to be like God without relying on His promise of welcome. She wanted to do it on her own—none of this "trust me; My love is enough" malarkey for her. She wanted to be proud of her accomplishments. She wanted to do it on her own.

Following in Eve's footsteps, Israel was also tempted by food. They wanted food that tasted better than the manna God was providing for them in the wilderness—food they could cook for themselves. "Give us some leeks and onions and some fish like we used to get in Egypt!" they moaned (see Numbers 11:5). They wanted food they could store away in case the Lord changed His mind about loving them or in case He forgot they needed to be fed. Besides, they were bored with the same old, same old. They wanted to exchange recipes for quail and lamb. They wanted to have competitions for best cook. They wanted to taste a little savory something in place of those dull honey wafers that fell outside their tent door every day.

We're just like the Israelites, aren't we? We want something more—some sure sign that we're okay after all and can finally feel satisfied in ourselves.

How did Jesus, our Brother, answer Satan's enticement? He said, "Man shall not live by bread alone, but by every word that comes from the mouth of God" (Matthew 4:4). Jesus found His complete life, rest, and identity in what God had to say about Him. He believed that His Father loved Him and would care for Him, no matter what He faced or how much He suffered.

None of us will find life by baking our own bread—or by trying to fulfill any of the ten thousand things we think we have to do to find self-acceptance, peace, rest, an answer to every question, and abundant life. But we keep trying, don't we? The mercies that God bestows on us every morning like manna outside our tents just seem too weak, too sweet, too boring (see Lamentations 3:22). There's just not enough *me* there. *Us* isn't good enough.

So how do we fight against our hunger for self-acceptance and self-approval? By hearing the good news and believing it—and then by hearing and believing it over and over again. By believing that we are already approved of. Here's a word from the mouth of God to remind us of this truth: "For our sake he made him to be sin who knew no sin, so that in him we might become the righteousness of God" (2 Corinthians 5:21). If you have the righteousness of God, isn't that enough?

Or do you need the righteousness of _____
(fill in your name) today?

In his second temptation, Satan tried to get Jesus to prove God's love for Jesus. "If you are the Son of God, throw yourself down," Satan hissed. "For it is written, 'He will command his angels concerning you,' and 'On their hands they will bear you up, lest you strike your foot against a stone'" (Matthew 4:6). Jesus didn't fall for that trick either. He knew without a doubt that His Father loved Him, but He didn't need His Father to prove it. He knew the promises of God's love in Scripture, and they were enough to convince Him that His Father would care for Him. Testing that love would be a sign of unbelief and idolatry.

Have you ever said, "I know God loves me, but I need something more—some tangible sign that I can feel"? If you need a sign that God loves you, you don't need to put out a fleece to prove it. He has already given us a sign—in fact, He has given us many. He has given us the sign of the rainbow— His promise to never destroy the world with water again. He has given us the sign of the Incarnation—the Messiah, who came to earth as a "baby wrapped in swaddling cloths and lying in a manger" (Luke 2:12). He has given us the sign of the Resurrection: "Just as Jonah was three days and three nights in the belly of the great fish, so will the Son of Man be three days and three nights in the heart of the earth" (Matthew 12:40).

These signs are assurances that God will keep His promise to care for us and that we don't need anything more than His word on it. The cross of Christ, that bloodied wood, is the surest sign any of us will ever need. Have our sins been for-given? Are we loved? Will He care for us? We need no more proof than to look to Golgotha and fall down in worship.

In his third temptation, Satan offered Jesus "all the king-doms of the world and their glory" (Matthew 4:8). Would Jesus succumb to the temptation to demand to be treated as a king, to be glorified as the ruler of all? No, of course not. Why not? Because He knew who He was. He already knew He was a King. He knew He was the Ruler of all the king-doms Satan offered Him. He knew what would happen one day: "At the name of Jesus every knee should bow, in heaven and on earth and under the earth, and every tongue confess that [he] is Lord, to the glory of God the Father" (Philippians 2:10-11).

Let's face it: our cravings for self-benediction and self-absolution have their roots in self-worship. We want to look with pride on all our little kingdoms and accomplishments. We want to be like God and understand everything. We want our own glory to fill the sky. As Paul Tripp says, "Sin has made us glory robbers."[43] Jesus, on the other hand, didn't need to rob anyone to get glory. He knew who He was and where He was going. He wasn't afraid that people wouldn't appreciate Him. And so He was able to say no to all the things we claw and strive for as we seek human approval.

If we don't know whether we have a good reputation in God's eyes (the only eyes that matter)—if we think we belong in the trash with the broken eggshells and the rot-ten vegetables—then we'll always be scratching and scraping, trying to find some way to feel okay. It's like this: if we've just finished a delicious steak dinner topped off with crème brûlée and a cup of rich coffee, we'll find it much easier to resist a little tin of Vienna wieners.

Do you know who you are in Him? Do you believe that you are loved just as you are? Then why would you need the kingdoms of this world and all their fading, empty glory? Listen to the words that God uses to describe you and believers everywhere: "You are a chosen race, a royal priesthood, a holy nation, a people for his own possession. . . . Once you were not a people, but now you are God's people; once you had not received mercy, but now you have received mercy" (1 Peter 2:9-10).

We are His treasured possession—we don't need anything more. We're not used-up, disease-ridden outcasts hoping to sneak by the really good people and steal some glory for ourselves. We already have everything we need, because He said *us*! We don't need to know every reason behind everything He allows. We know Him, and we know He welcomes and loves us.

Christ's Reputation—and Ours

When we talk about the righteousness of Christ—about how He fulfilled the entire law for us, in our place—what does that actually mean? It means that every day of His entire life, He chose to love His Father and His neighbor—for us, in our place. When Jesus was a child and His little brother cheated at a game, He didn't slug him. He loved him. When He was a teenager and the village girls flirted with Him, He

For years I've been fed the lie that my marriage will fall apart if my husband doesn't fit the traditional role of spiritual leader. I made him feel guilty for not being spiritual enough, and this caused him to fake where he was in his faith. This stunted his spiritual growth and mine, because I was leaning on him for my spirituality and not growing myself. Eventually God helped me let go of my expectations, and over time my husband and I started growing spiritually in our own genuine ways.

One Woman's STORY

didn't view them as objects for His own pleasure. He loved them and cared for them the way a big brother cares for and protects a little sister. When His earthly father died, He stepped into the role of the head of His household without complaint and supported His siblings and His mother until His dying breath, when He gave her over to the care of His best friend, John.[44]

When the disciples tried to snatch Jesus' glory or push others aside, He loved them and assured them that they would indeed have a Kingdom—just not the one they expected. Then, when He was stripped naked and shamed and beaten and nailed to a tree, when He no longer had the assurance of His Father's presence, He still called His Father "my God" and asked that anguished question, "Why have you forsaken me?" (Mark 15:34).

And in His final breath, when He said, "It is finished" (John 19:30), He was saying it for *us*. Yes, He was finishing the work His Father had given Him to do, but He was also finishing all that we had to do in order to hear God's gracious benediction, to win His favor.

What kind of righteousness did Jesus earn? What was His reputation? What did He think of Himself? He said that He "always" did what was pleasing to His Father (John 8:29). Think of that. He never went to bed with a guilty conscience. He never looked back on His day with chagrin, wishing He could take something back and start over again. He never groaned inside with consciousness of sin or looked back at a time during His life with shame and sorrow. His entire time on earth was so focused on doing the will of His Father that His Father's will was like His food (see John 4:34). When He was confronted with circumstances that called for judgment, He knew His judgment was always right, because He never sought His own will but only the will of His Father (see John 5:30).

Jesus' life was so perfect (without being priggish) that He could ask this astonishing question: "Which one of you convicts me of sin?" (John 8:46). Who would dare to ask such a question? I certainly wouldn't. There are things in my past (and in my present) that should not be there—things I'm ashamed of. But Jesus, the One who is here for us and with us, could ask it without fear. And He could say that Satan had "no hold" over Him (John 14:30, NIV). As hard as the devil tried, none of his temptations were successful. Satan had no claim on Jesus, because Jesus knew that He was loved, and therefore He loved in return.

Jesus was clear about the reason He had come: "Do not think that I have come to abolish the Law or the Prophets; I have not come to abolish them but to fulfill them. For truly, I say to you, until heaven and earth pass away, not an iota, not a dot, will pass from the Law until all is accomplished" (Matthew 5:17-18).

He came to fulfill all the commandments of the law. As a result, He subjected Himself to all the consequences described by the prophets. Every time a law promised, "Do this and you will be blessed and live" or warned, "Fail to obey and you be cursed and die,"[45] He stood in our place. He was thinking about us. Jesus obeyed, fulfilling the law for us, so that His blessing would be ours. Every prophecy that foretold destruction on the disobedient, Jesus bore for us in His body. He bore the curse of the law for disobedience on that cursed tree, for "cursed is everyone who is hanged on a tree" (Galatians 3:13). And He fulfilled even the tiniest detail of the moral law so that we could know with certainty that we stand righteous before the Father, who sees us as we really are and yet calls us "beloved."

The apostle John wrote of our adoption as God's beloved children in this way: "See what kind of love the Father has given to us, that we should be called children of God; and so we are. . . . Beloved, we are God's children now" (1 John 3:1-2). Paul, too, referred to us as "beloved children" (Ephesians 5:1).

That testimony Jesus gave about His own life is now the

testimony of our lives. Because we are with Him, we have the record of always doing what is pleasing to the Father. Because Jesus lived righteously for us, we have the testimony of having God's will be the food that sustains us. That means we can look at the enemy—and even at the Father—and say, "Because I am in the Son, who could ever convict me of sin?"

Do we still sin? Yes, of course we do. But when it comes to our standing before the holy Judge of the universe, He will not convict us of sin. Why? Because in His eyes, we are forgiven, righteous, and clean. There's nothing in us that will keep us from Him or Him from us. We are with the Son, and He has given us everything we need. It's no longer just Jesus who is righteous—it's *us*.

In light of such good news, why would we ever try to build our own résumé or think we need Him to explain anything to us?

A Sweet Tearing Open

At Jesus' baptism, the Father tore open the heavens and came down to pronounce this benediction on His Son: "You are my beloved Son; with you I am well pleased" (Luke 3:22). Three and a half years passed—years of service and teaching and signs and friendship and suffering—and then it was time for another tearing. This was a tearing that would change everything forever.

When the Son's soul was torn from His body and His final act of obedience was complete, the curtain in the Temple that had separated people from God, keeping sinful human beings from God's holiness, was torn. It was rent completely, from top to bottom (see Matthew 27:51). It was as though God Himself had reached down from the heavens and ripped the curtain in half.

Do you need proof—some sign that God counts you as righteous? When He tore that curtain down the middle, He was saying, "You're home now. Come in. You are welcome in My presence! Don't stand far away, hoping I will accept you. My Son has done it all for you, and I'm fully satisfied in your righteousness. I will never condemn you for your sin!"

The way is open now, and there is no reason for us to tremble or hope we're good enough or try to build our reputation. The Son's body was broken, and the curtain was torn in two. That means we can approach Him in confidence:

> We have confidence to enter the holy places by the blood of Jesus, by the new and living way that he opened for us through the curtain, that is, through his flesh. . . . Let us draw near with a true heart in full assurance of faith, with our hearts sprinkled clean from an evil conscience and our bodies washed with pure water. Let us hold fast the confession of our hope without wavering, for he who promised is faithful. HEBREWS 10:19-20, 22-23

Right now, just as we are, we are the Father's beloved daughters and sons (see 1 John 3:2). Do you need a reminder of that truth as you look in the mirror? Here it is: *God calls me His beloved daughter. Who can convict me of sin? Who can condemn me?* Romans 8:31-35 puts it this way:

If God is for us, who can be against us? He who did not spare his own Son but gave him up for us all, how will he not also with him graciously give us all things? Who shall bring any charge against God's elect? It is God who justifies. Who is to condemn? Christ Jesus is the one who died—more than that, who was raised—who is at the right hand of God, who indeed is interceding for us. Who shall separate us from the love of Christ?

So what do we do about the mess we're in? We give it to Him, believing He will take care of it all. We trust that even though we may not understand everything, He loves us and will care for us forever. The way is open. The summons has been issued: *Come home. Know that He welcomes you and loves you.* His righteousness doesn't cover Him alone. It's for us!

Questions FOR REFLECTION AND DISCUSSION

1. Lamentations 3:22-24 says, "The steadfast love of the LORD never ceases; his mercies never come to an end; they are new every morning; great is your faithfulness. 'The LORD is my portion,' says my soul, 'therefore I will hope in him.'" What do you think it means that the Lord is your portion? How have you seen His steadfast love and faithfulness in your life? How does the truth that His love never ceases encourage you when you face troubling circumstances?

2. Scripture says, "Christ also suffered once for sins, the righteous for the unrighteous, that he might bring us to God" (1 Peter 3:18). What do you think this means in the big picture? What does it mean for you personally?

3. Australian theologian Graeme Goldsworthy said, "The sinner who believes God's word that this redemptive act is for him is given, as a free gift, the same status that Christ possesses by virtue of his sin-free obedience. We cannot say it better than to use Paul's words: 'Christ, who is our life' (Colossians 3:4)."[46] Do you agree that you possess Christ's sin-free obedience? Do you always feel that to be true?

4. Paul wrote, "Oh, the depth of the riches and wisdom and knowledge of God! How unsearchable are his judgments and how inscrutable his ways! 'For who has known the mind of the Lord, or who has been his counselor?'" (Romans 11:33-34). How might these words comfort you when you're faced with a situation you don't understand?

5. Do you believe it's possible that, because of your faith in Christ's work for you, God won't condemn you for any sin? How might this affect your efforts to seek out more and better rules for improving your life?

6. Summarize what you've learned in this chapter in four or five sentences.

CHAPTER 8

WHAT'S ON *HIS* LIST
FOR YOU TODAY?

As LONG AS WE LIVE here on earth, the voices clamoring to
fill our ears with bad news will not be silenced. There will
never be an end to the rules from both culture ("Be beautiful!" "Be strong!" "Be competent!" "Grab the good life!")
and the church ("Do more!" "Serve more!" "Do better!"
"Be better!").

As long as we are conscious and breathing, we will be
bombarded with messages of self-justification: "I'm okay!"
or "Maybe I'm not okay, but I'm not as bad as _____!"
or "Maybe I'm not okay, but it's not my fault!" or "All right,
I know I'm not okay, but I'm going to get better!"

These messages about our own okay-ness are not
the gospel. As Christians, we don't need to try to justify

ourselves. The gospel is about broken people who are not simply "not okay" but who are more sinful and flawed than we ever dared believe.[47] And although we know in our heads that we should ignore worldly ways of thinking, it's something we have to work on all the time. Romans 12:2 offers this admonition, which is as relevant today as it was when Paul wrote it: "Do not be conformed to this world, but be transformed by the renewal of your mind, that by testing you may discern what is the will of God, what is good and acceptable and perfect" (Romans 12:2).

Being "conformed to this world" simply means that we value and adhere to the world's ways of thinking. And while, of course, that means we should shun immoral lifestyles, it also means we should turn away from the methods the world uses to seek self-justification. The world's message sounds something like this: "If you do this [whatever *this* may be], you will be happy, at peace, loved, and able to approve of yourself." If we buy into this way of thinking, we accept the lies Satan started spinning in Eden and continues telling to this day. When you feel the impulse to do more and try harder and keep up with the Joneses down the street (or the Angelinas on the magazine covers), you'll know that the world is forcing you into its mold. Self-perfectionism is the world's way of doing business.

Rather than be forced into worldly ways of thinking, we are to be "transformed by the renewal" of our minds. That means that we need to remember the gospel every day: we are already loved, already perfected, already approved of, already justified. We don't need to try to justify ourselves by what we do or how we look, or assure ourselves that we're okay because of the progress we're making.

There was a time in my life when the kind of car I drove was overly important to me. I really thought that if I drove a Volvo station wagon, people would think I was a woman of substance, not just some gal faking respectability. On one day in particular, I remember dropping off my preschoolers at a little community day care and feeling as though I didn't measure up to the other women. In that moment, I looked outside at my Volvo and thought, *I hope they see me get into my car.* I know that's ridiculous, but underneath that thought was my fear that people would discover what a sham I was. At that point in my life I didn't know that I needed to just relax into the truth that I was indeed a sham, just like everyone else, and that the only goodness I had was goodness that came from Someone else.

My thinking needed renovation; the Holy Spirit needed to build a new identity in me. I didn't know who I was or what made me unique and uniquely loved. I had a hard time accepting that I was worthy of being loved in those days, and I frequently worried, spent too much money, and battled feelings of anger. I constantly looked to my husband to give me his "respectable" identity. I needed my home, my car, and my clothing to declare something about me that I didn't really believe myself. I wanted to be welcomed and loved. I didn't realize I was already welcomed and loved—just the way I was. The Lord needed to help me "set [my] hope fully on the grace that will be brought to [me] at the revelation of Jesus Christ" (1 Peter 1:13).

This is what I wish I'd known about lists and steps back then—the only list that really matters.

What's on His List for You Today?

1. Resist the world's ways of thinking.

It's time to turn off the incessant siren call of commercials, billboards, magazine headlines, and media advice about how we can perfect ourselves. It's time to "set [our] hope fully on the grace . . . of Jesus Christ" (1 Peter 1:13).

This process of tuning out the world's chatter may look different for each person and each family, but in my household it means that when we watch TV, we mute or fast-forward through the commercials. This is one time when technology makes it easier to battle temptation: we record nearly every program we watch, which makes it easier to avoid having people tell us what we must buy so we, too, can be beautiful, smiling, and glamorous. Anyone older than six years old knows that getting a new toy doesn't give us instant happiness or popularity or peace. Right? But we're more easily swayed than we'd like to believe.

It's not just the commercials, either. When *Extreme Makeover: Home Edition* first aired, my husband, Phil, and I loved to watch it. And while the work that was being done to help people in distress was good, it wasn't good for me. I kept looking around at my house, thinking, *This place needs a face-lift too,* which resulted in our spending a big chunk of change on remodeling. Now, I'm not saying that people should never spend money on their homes or that the work wasn't ultimately a blessing for our family. It's just that if I had never watched that show, I probably wouldn't have felt the discontentment that prompted our remodeling—or the urgency to make it happen right away.

The show *What Not to Wear* influences me in a similar way. I've noticed that after I watch it, I'm swifter to judge other women by the way they dress, and I'm more prone to frantically run to the mall to try to buy something new (even though my closets are already full).

I'm amazed at how easily influenced I am. When I watch programs that portray people who are hopeless, cynical, envious, and self-indulgent, I find myself acting the same way. And while it feels relaxing to spend time in front of the television, it eventually results in further confusion and self-condemnation.

Am I laying down yet another rule for women to follow? No, of course not. I'm simply reminding all of us to be aware of the ways the media influences us and how, despite a promise of rest and relaxation, it actually wears down our overburdened souls even more. When we listen to the voices of the world, we are less able to discern God's will (which is good, acceptable, and perfect) because our hearts are being torn in a thousand different directions. When we listen to the voices of the world, we are bombarded with images of how life should look, and we're fooled into thinking we need something more to be okay. We wrestle with the constant suspicion that something important is missing—that some key to a great life is just around the corner—but we can never find it. And then, when the day comes to a close, all the time

Bad Advice WOMEN RECEIVE

What are the dumbest things people tell women they have to do in order to be godly?

(These are real responses to the question I posted on Facebook.)

- Make sure you know how to craft, cook delicious meals, decorate your home beautifully, and throw fabulous parties. This is how you, as a woman, reflect the image of God—by displaying beauty.
- Have a "full quiver"—that is, have as many babies as physically possible.
- Never have authority over any man, in any context.
- Avoid makeup, tattoos, and piercings—they are the "uniform of the enemy." Don't wear high heels—they are immodest.
- Don't talk about theology with other women, because that's where people tend to get "off track."

we spent in front of the screen (any screen) only adds to the guilt we feel.

The same holds true for social media. Don't allow the beautiful pictures that your friends post on Facebook or on Instagram fool you into thinking that anyone else's life is happier or easier or shinier than yours. I recently heard my friend Pastor Tullian Tchividjian confess publicly that there have been times when his family has been at one another's throats

- If you're having marital problems, it's because you are not submitting.
- Smile even when things are bad so people will see the "joy of the Lord."
- Women shouldn't go to seminary. They should get married and let their husband teach them.
- If your husband is making a bad decision, keep your mouth shut—that makes you submissive. You're not being his helper if you offer a different perspective.
- Try harder.

THE *Good News*

To the one who works, his wages are not counted as a gift but as his due. And to the one who does not work but believes in him who justifies the ungodly, his faith is counted as righteousness. ROMANS 4:4-5

but then has stopped to take a smiling picture to post to Twitter. He's not alone. Social media is a good way to get good news out, but it is also a good way to propagate envy, discontent, despair, and loneliness. No matter how many "friends" like something you post or favorite one of your tweets, it's not the same thing as investing in a face-to-face relationship.

I recently read a Facebook post from a young woman who claimed to have it all together. She boasted that she was a great (and oh-so-happy) mom, that she had three remarkably wonderful children, that they had just spent an amazing day shopping on a limited budget, and that they had gotten home in time to make a nutritious dinner for dear Hubby before they spent a fun family night together. Seriously? When we read stuff like that, how are we supposed to respond? We fall into envy or despair, or we determine to try harder tomorrow because, after all, if she can do it, so can we. Sometimes I wish that every once in a while people would post or tweet about how messed up they are and how they're relying on Christ alone. Now *that* would encourage me.

No matter what we do to make ourselves look like Ms. Facebook Perfect, we'll never be able to justify ourselves, because we can't. No mere mortal woman can justify herself, because we are all sinners and God isn't fooled by our disingenuously smiling selfies. We can't justify ourselves because it's not our job. The job of justifier has already been filled. It's our job to remember that we have been declared justified. We are already forgiven; we are already righteous.

What's on His list for you today? Be renewed by the transformation of your mind as you ponder all He has already done for you. *Remember the gospel.*

2. Resist legalistic messages from the church.

The world isn't the only source that broadcasts neverending rules into our hearts and minds. Sadly, the church also voices messages of self-improvement to us—and these messages are difficult to ignore because they are tangled up with actual commands from the Bible. Since we want to live in grateful obedience for our salvation, messages that come from Christian speakers and writers have more power to condemn us. So when we hear rules about what we should do to please God, we need to be good students of the Bible. We need to ask ourselves, *Is this actually something that the Bible specifically commands?* We should also ask, *Is this a wise application of specific verses?* If the answer isn't a resounding yes, then we can feel free to ignore it.

For instance, in the paragraphs above, I suggested that one of the ways we might wisely apply the teaching of Romans 12:2 is by limiting our time in front of a television screen. Because this is not a direct command from God, you are free to ignore my perspective. The Bible doesn't say anything about how much time we may spend in front of a screen, so I don't have the authority to bind your conscience in any way. If you choose to make a different choice, you are free to do so without fear. You know your heart, your schedule, and the way you respond to the circumstances in your life better than I do. So unplug if you think it will be good for you. Plug in if you think it doesn't matter. Although I've tried to be wise and measured in my counsel to you, I'm applying a broad passage in a specific way, and the only One with the authority to demand that you obey is God.

In addition, much of the advice we've heard from the church over the past couple of decades has taken Scripture and twisted it to fit our cultural norms. Because God has uniquely blessed marriage and the family, some people in the church have taken that to mean that family—particularly a woman's role in her family—is her only calling.

But the messages of "Be a perfect mom" and "Be a perfect woman" are not the gospel. This is not good news. This is a false message of self-salvation, and it is not what Jesus has to say to us. Jesus was no chauvinist. He loved women. He didn't tell women to spend their days worrying about whether they looked good enough for their husbands or making perfectly balanced organic lunches. He wasn't looking for a trophy wife who would enhance His reputation or for a supermom who posted the best crafts on Pinterest. Jesus told women that He loved them and that they could rest in Him.

What's on His list for you today? He wants you to judge whether something you're hearing is from the Lord by asking questions like these: "Is this something Jesus would say to me? Was He concerned about such things? Would this rule work in a different culture or time?" *Remember the gospel.*

3. Ask yourself, "Is what I'm fretting over eternal?"

We need to remember that our standing with God is based not on our punctilious responses to man-made rules but rather on our faith in the obedience of Another. Please don't pile more guilt on yourself about how you look or how well organized your closets are or any other earthly measuring stick. All these things will perish. We will grow old. Our skin will wrinkle. Someday the next generation will have to empty our closets and take all the junk we fussed over to the Salvation Army. Everything here on earth will ultimately burn. These things will not produce hearts that are filled with the "imperishable beauty of a gentle and quiet spirit" (1 Peter 3:4).

In the Sermon on the Mount, Jesus addressed the topic of worry in depth. He equated worry with earthly treasure:

> Do not lay up for yourselves treasures on earth, where moth and rust destroy and where thieves break in and steal, but lay up for yourselves treasures in heaven, where neither moth nor rust destroys and where thieves do not break in and steal. For where your treasure is, there your heart will be also. . . . But seek first the kingdom of God and his righteousness, and all these things will be added to you.
>
> MATTHEW 6:19-21, 33

Worry and anxiety are the hallmarks of lives focused on building our own little kingdoms. Whenever we make something here on earth our treasure, we're going to drown in worry. Why? Because everything we have here will burn—or be eaten by moths or destroyed by rust or stolen by thieves.

That means we have to guard our hearts against making anything here on earth overly important. We might turn our families or our jobs into our kingdoms; we might make our plans for a peaceful home our treasure. Certainly, there's nothing wrong with a strong family, profitable employment, or a peace-filled home, but we get into trouble when we make those things the measure of our identity. They become our treasure when we use them to give ourselves worth.

Notice that Jesus' command doesn't stop with words about treasuring the little fiefdoms we're all so prone to build. His command also includes a warning against seeking our own righteousness. He knows our tendency—that we're way too prone to seek after our own righteousness. After all, that's why we take in all the rules, to-do lists, and bad advice—we want to approve of ourselves and assure ourselves that we are okay after all.

So what's on His list for you to do today? Resist all the voices that lie to you and tell you that God wants you to do more and try harder. Rest your heart in His perfections. Listen for His voice. For it is only then that you'll be able to do good without fearing "anything that is frightening" (1 Peter 3:6).

What's on His list for you to do today? *Remember the gospel.*

4. Live transparently.

If it is true that we are all sinners in need of grace, and if, most happily, Jesus loves sinners, then why don't we all stop pretending to be something other than what we are? One of the reasons we are so weary is because we waste so much effort to keep our masks in place. It's why we are so driven. It's why we can't rest or admit our own weaknesses or let others see us as we really are. It's why we feel so threatened when we are criticized and why we toss and turn at night rehearsing our failures from the day. It's why we post faux pictures of how happy we are, how great our toenails look after our pedicures, how scrumptious our desserts look.

We never post pictures of how we can't zip up our pants or status updates about how we cried right after that photo was snapped or how we scavenge the medicine cabinet each night looking for something to take the edge off. We

Growing up in "Christian culture," I received a lot of messages that God wants nothing more from us than to be "good." We're to be models of perfection, hide our flaws, and work really hard to earn the love of the people around us and God. What I'm learning now, however, is that the message of Jesus in the Gospels isn't so much about washing your hands before you eat or making things look good by following external rules. It's more about doing right to be more like Him and to live in closer alignment with Him. Recently I've started to feel the desire to submit to Jesus and not be so consumed with what other people think of me.

One Woman's
-—∾ STORY ∾—-

are afraid that we aren't worthy of the love that has been given to us, and so we stuff our fear and inadequacies deep inside. But while it's true that on our own we have nothing to recommend us, God has nevertheless lavished His love upon us.

In light of that truth, we can live transparent lives and encourage other women to do so as well. We can freely confess our weaknesses and sins to one another. We can take off our perfect-church-lady masks, knowing that our failures no longer define us. Rather, we are defined by the perfect life of One who lived two thousand years ago and the blood He poured out in our place.

As I've had the opportunity and privilege to travel around the nation speaking at women's conferences, one of the constant refrains I hear is, "Thank you for being so real. Thank you for letting me know I'm not the only one who is weak." While I'm grateful for these responses, it also breaks my heart. Shouldn't our churches be the one place where we are free to be who we really are—sinners in need of a Savior? Shouldn't Christian women feel at ease confessing our weakness and sin to one another, because weakness and sin aren't the only words that define our identity? Doesn't claiming Christianity mean we know we need a Savior and we believe He has been provided for us?

Our sin is bad news only if we don't have a Savior. But we do have one, and He has promised that all our sins have already been cleansed (see 2 Peter 1:9; Revelation 7:14). We have the "righteousness of God" right now (Romans 3:22). A day is coming when we will be with Him, completely free from our weakness and sin, and ever so grateful for the grace that has sustained us during this long journey.

What's on His list for you today? Live your life transparently so other women will see that Jesus loves the weak, the weary, the wounded, and the sinner, and perhaps they, too, will be emboldened to stop faking it.

And while you're at it, laugh a lot. Take a good look at all the people Jesus calls *holy*, *chosen*, *royal*, and *precious*, and don't stifle your giggle. Laugh because He is strong enough to use the broken to build His church. Stop looking at the people in the Bible as heroes to pattern your life after. Don't try to be like Moses or Mary. Don't dare to be a Daniel. Rather, fall on your face before the sinless One and rejoice. After all, there is only one Hero in the Bible—and He's all we need.

Look at the people in the Bible and smile, because God, in His infinite wisdom, has made it plain that no one, aside from the Son, is worthy of the title *beloved* . . . and yet that's what He calls us! We are the beloved daughters with whom He is well pleased. So laugh at yourself as you begin to see the joke He's telling through your brokenness.

We have been called to help other women give up their masks and walk into transparency, vulnerability, and authenticity. That's what John was talking about when he said, "If we walk in the light, as he is in the light, we have fellowship with one another, and the blood of Jesus his Son cleanses us from all sin. If we say we have no sin, we deceive ourselves, and the truth is not in us" (1 John 1:7-8).

Walking in the light simply means that we open up our lives to the light of His Word and let it pierce our hearts, shining deeply into all the secret corners where we still don't believe He's enough, and then letting the truth of His love and His welcome expose and transform us. This can happen only when we're ourselves—not when we're pretending to be something other than what we are. Sin is never banished in the dark. Rather, we are transformed when we admit who we are and then rest in all He has done for us.

What's on His list for you today? Take a good long look at yourself and laugh at God's sense of humor in calling you a saint. And while you're at it, admit the truth about yourself to someone else—that person knows it anyway. And then you two can chuckle together and rejoice in grace. *Remember the gospel.*

5. Submit.

As women, we've heard a lot of messages about submission, haven't we? We've heard that all Christians are to submit to one another "out of reverence for Christ" (Ephesians 5:21). We've heard that wives are to take on positions of submission to their husbands' servant-leadership (see Ephesians 5:22). We've also heard that both women and men are to submit to their leaders in the church (see Hebrews 13:17) and in the civic government (Romans 13:1). I am glad for these teachings.

But I wonder how many women (or men) have been taught that the primary submission we need to seek more than anything else is submission to God's righteousness. How many Mother's Day sermons have you heard about how you should rest from your many labors and submit to the imputed righteousness of Christ?

Let's keep talking about submission in relationships, but let's talk even more about submission to His plan to grant righteousness to us so we no longer have to strive after a "righteousness that is based on the law" (Romans 10:5). Why? Because the woman who seeks to establish her own righteousness, her okay-ness, by keeping the law is under the curse of disobedience. She simply can't do it.

This is what true submission requires: "With the heart one believes and is justified, and with the mouth one confesses and is saved. . . . For there is no distinction between Jew and Greek; for the same Lord is Lord of all, bestowing his riches on all who call on him. For *'everyone who calls on the name of the Lord will be saved'*" (Romans 10:10, 12-13, emphasis added).

What does it take to submit? It takes humility. It takes a childlike heart that says, *I can't do this, Daddy. Will you help me?* It takes coming to the end of ourselves in exhaustion and despair. It takes a death to our "I'm going to gut this out and prove that I'm okay after all" heart. And it is there, right in the middle of our assumption that all is lost and we're bound for perdition, that we are closest to grace. From there, real righteousness is just a call away. Call on the name of the Lord, and you will be saved!

What's on His list for you today? Submit to His righteousness. *Remember the gospel.*

6. Put the law in its place.

In light of all I've said against to-do lists, steps, and bad advice, you might wonder if I'm saying we should live our lives any old way we please. After all, if the grace and justification Jesus has brought to us are so potent, then maybe we don't need to be concerned about sin at all. If you're asking that question, let me tell you that you're not the only person who has. Paul's detractors asked the same thing when they heard about the astonishing declaration of God's grace for those who had ignored the law written on their consciences

Godly Ways TO DEAL WITH FAILURE

What are some healthy ways you're learning to respond to feelings of failure?

(The following responses were gathered from focus groups.)

- I am starting to learn that I can give it to Jesus, believing there is love and hope and freedom in Him, regardless of my failures and what the world says about me. He offers me a new start.
- I get cagey and feel trapped at first, but eventually I fall exhausted at the feet of my Savior. I know He wants my heart, not my works.
- For years I responded by shutting down. In the past year I have been learning that my failure is a chance for me to grow and learn. My first instinct is to shut up and give up, but after a few deep breaths and maybe some tears, I begin to lean into God. I have caught myself saying, "God, who is going to save me from this mess?" And then I realize, *Oh right, Your Son already did that!*
- I'm trying to turn to God at the beginning, not just when I hit the bottom of my emotions. I'm learning to acknowledge that I can't do it alone and that I need Him every minute.

(the Gentiles) and those who had ignored the Law given to them from Mount Sinai (the Jews).

Here's how Paul framed their question: "Are we to con-

- I cry out to the Lord, tearfully asking Him to get me through.
- I ask my husband or close friends or even my kids to pray for me.
- I am learning to focus on the eternal value of my choices.
- I make sure I'm in healthy community with other Christian women.
- Sometimes I go for a drive alone, listening to music, praying silently, or crying out to the Lord.
- I preach the gospel to myself. I acknowledge that I'm perfect because of Christ, not because of my behavior. Because of Jesus, God is pleased with me.
- I surrender to Jesus, saying, "I believe! Help my unbelief!"
- I ask Jesus to reveal the distortion in my heart, to point out the wrong view of God that leads me to feel like a failure. I am not a failure because He is not a failure, and I am hidden in Him.
- I used to text friends and ask for their counsel first. Now I'm starting to talk to Jesus first and foremost. If there are lies, I write them down and put them side by side with His truth.
- By God's grace, my eyes are being opened to who God is, who I am in light of His character, and how He has forgiven me.

tinue in sin that grace may abound?" (Romans 6:1). In other words, should those of us who have trusted in Christ, who have tasted His grace in spite of our sin, just throw ourselves into more and more sin so that He can show off how great His grace is? After all, if God is glorified by showering grace on sinners, then wouldn't He receive even more glory if He showered grace on bigger sinners?

Paul didn't equivocate in his answer to their question. He issued a strong renunciation of such a thought. "By no means!" he replied (Romans 6:2). The truth is that the message of the gospel should never produce in us an indifferent attitude to God's law. Rather, the message of God's grace should make us more desirous of obedience, not less. But the law must never be allowed to make us think that God is sitting up in heaven, impatiently tapping His toe, waiting for us to get our acts together. The message of what our Savior has done for us should motivate us to desire to live in grateful compliance to His will.

Paul tells us, "Christ is the end of the law for righteousness to everyone who believes" (Romans 10:4). Do we seek to obey the law of God? Yes, of course—but only because we are grateful for what Christ has already done for us, not because we're trying to earn merit or appease him.

What is on His list for you today? Live in grateful obedience, knowing that even when you fail, you are still forgiven, righteous, and loved. The law no longer has the power to condemn you. Keep it out of your conscience, but let it guide the way you respond to His love. *Remember the gospel.*

7. Know who you really are.
We are in union with Jesus. When He died on Calvary in payment for sin, we died there with Him. And if it's true that

we died with Him, we can know that we will also be raised with Him. Our slavery to sin has been broken. That doesn't mean that we will never struggle against sin again or that the struggle won't be desperate at times. But it does mean that sin's power to condemn us, to fill us with obedience-depleting guilt, is over.

Now when we sin, rather than fall into a pit of self-condemnation and guilt, we can look up and say, "Thank You, Lord, for reminding me once again of my need for a Savior and of how You suffered in my place. Thank You that You have freed me from the power of guilt and made me Your beloved child. Thank You that the punishment of death for sin will never overtake me. I believe that right now, even in my failures, I live for You. Please enable me to continue to believe the gospel, no matter how I fail."

What's on His list for you today? Remember who you already are! You have new life. You have been resurrected from your old, dead life, just as Jesus was raised from the dead by the glory of the Father. *Remember the gospel.*

8. Accept that you are new.

This is the glorious good news: we are new. Yes, we should seek to obey the Lord's Word to us, but we should never allow ourselves to be placed back in slavery to man-made rules in order to earn God's blessing. The Kingdom of God is not a man-made meritocracy. It is a Kingdom ruled by the gracious generosity of the King, who has done everything and given all for us.

We are new. We no longer have to prove our worth and

try to assuage the guilt feelings of our own consciences. We seek to live lives that are pleasing to the Lord, but we do so only because He has already made us pleasing to Him.

We are new. We can lay our heads on the pillow at night and thank Him that in all our failures (and in all our successes), we have His love, forgiveness, and smile. And we can pray for grace to believe and obey tomorrow.

We are new. Rather than compare ourselves to others, thinking they are more or less holy than we are, we can rejoice that the Lord has already spoken "righteous" over us and that He will incline our hearts to get us to where we need to be, when we need to be there.

We are new. We no longer have to seek to justify ourselves by looking a certain way, eating a certain way, marching for a certain cause, or giving birth to a certain number of children. We no longer have to justify ourselves, because we are already justified.

We are new. We no longer have to strive to forgive ourselves, because we've already been forgiven by the only Person whose opinion matters.

This reminder from Graeme Goldsworthy will help equip us to fight all those messages about the rules we need to fulfill in order to be righteous:

> All the fruits of the gospel are just that: fruits *of the gospel*. Regeneration, faith, sanctification and final perseverance are all fruits of the gospel. They can grow on no other tree. Legalistic demands, cajolery, and browbeatings for "deeper commitment" and

"total surrender," when cut loose from the grace of the gospel are but wretched weeds which can produce only despondency, disillusionment and rebelliousness.[48]

What's on His list for you today? *Remember the gospel.*

The Final Benediction

Hear and believe that this word of blessing from the Lord is for you: "The LORD bless you and keep you; the LORD make his face to shine upon you and be gracious to you; the LORD lift up his countenance upon you and give you peace" (Numbers 6:24-26). Here's the good news for your weary soul: you don't have to do anything more than believe the gospel for God to smile upon you. You already have His blessing, His protection, His grace, and the promise of deep peace. It's all yours already. You can rest from your labor.

[Jesus said,] "Come to me, all who labor and are heavy laden, and I will give you rest." MATTHEW 11:28

Questions FOR REFLECTION AND DISCUSSION

1. In many places throughout Scripture, God refers to His people as His "possession" or "treasured possession" (Exodus 19:5; Deuteronomy 7:6; 14:2; 26:18; Titus 2:14). What does it mean to you that even though you aren't perfectly obedient, Christ's

work on your behalf has made you God's treasured possession?

2. Look back over the list of eight things laid out for you in this chapter. Which are most meaningful to you? Which ones will you begin doing today?

3. Take another look at the "Accept that you are new" section. When is it most difficult for you to believe that God has made you new? When have you experienced a true glimpse of being made new?

4. Read Matthew 11:28-30: "Come to me, all who labor and are heavy laden, and I will give you rest. Take my yoke upon you, and learn from me, for I am gentle and lowly in heart, and you will find rest for your souls. For my yoke is easy, and my burden is light." What does Jesus mean when He says that His "yoke is easy" and His "burden is light"? How has Christ given you rest?

5. Summarize what you have learned in this chapter in four or five sentences.

6. Summarize what you have learned in this book. If a friend asked you what this book was about, what would you say? If you had to present on this book to a group of seventh-grade girls (yipes!), what would you say?

THE BEST NEWS EVER

I DIDN'T BEGIN to understand the gospel until the summer before my twenty-first birthday. Although I had attended church and Sunday school occasionally in my childhood, it never really transformed me in any significant way. I knew, without really understanding, the importance of Christmas and Easter. I remember looking at the beautiful stained-glass windows, with their cranberry red and deep cerulean blue, and as I took in the image of Jesus knocking on a garden door, I had a vague sense that being religious was a good thing. But I didn't have the foggiest idea about the gospel. I'm quite sure that wasn't the fault of those sweet Sunday school teachers—it was just that my heart hadn't been softened to the gospel yet.

During adolescence, I was consistently in trouble, and I hated everyone who pointed that out. I was constantly filled with anger and despair. There were nights when I prayed that I would be good or, more specifically, that I would get out of whatever trouble I was in. I would ask God to help me do better, only to be disappointed by my failures the following day.

At age seventeen, just after graduating from high school, I got married. All before the third decade of my life began, I'd gotten married, had a baby, and gotten divorced. In the months and years that followed, I discovered the anesthetizing effects of drugs, alcohol, and illicit relationships. Although I was known as a girl who liked to party, I was utterly lost and joyless, and I was beginning to realize it.

At one point, I remember telling a friend that I felt as if I was fifty years old, which, at that point in my life, was the oldest I could even imagine being. I was exhausted and disgusted, so I decided to set about improving myself. I worked a full-time job, took a full course load at a local junior college, and cared for my son. I changed my living arrangements and tried to start over. I didn't know that the Holy Spirit was working in my heart, calling me to the Son. I just knew that something had to change. I was still living a shamefully wicked life; it's just that I was beginning to wake up to a different possibility.

At this point, Julie entered my life. She was my next-door neighbor, and she was a Christian. She was kind to me, and we became fast friends. She had a quality of life that attracted me, and she was always talking to me about her Savior, Jesus.

She let me know that she was praying for me and would frequently encourage me to "get saved." Although I'd heard about that in Sunday school, what she had to say seemed completely different from what I'd remembered hearing. She told me I needed to be born again.

And so, on a warm night in June of 1971, I knelt down in my tiny apartment and told the Lord that I wanted to be His. At that point, I didn't really understand much about the gospel, but I did understand this: I was desperate, and I desperately believed that the Lord would help me. That prayer on that night changed everything. I remember it now, forty-three years later, as if it were yesterday.

I knew I needed to be saved, and I trusted that Christ could save me. Similarly, one man who came in contact with some of Jesus' followers asked the question, "What must I do to be saved?" The answer was simple: "Believe in the Lord Jesus, and you will be saved" (Acts 16:30-31).

What do you need to do in order to be a Christian? There are only two things you need to believe. First, you need to know that you need salvation, help, and deliverance. You must not try to reform yourself or decide that you're going to become a moral person so God will be impressed. Because He is completely holy—that is, perfectly moral— you have to give up any idea that you can be good enough to meet His standard. That's the good bad news. It's bad news because it confirms you're in an impossible situation you can't change. But it's also good news, because it frees you from endless cycles of self-improvement that ultimately end in failure.

And the bad news leads you to the good news that Jesus has already done what you can't do for yourself. He lived a perfectly holy life on your behalf. This is the gospel. Basically, the gospel is the story of how God looked down through the corridors of time and set His love on His people. At a specific point in time, He sent His Son into the world to become fully like us.

This is the story we hear about at Christmas. This baby grew to be a man, and after thirty years of obscurity, Jesus began to show people who He was. He did this by performing miracles, healing the sick, and raising the dead. He also demonstrated His deity by teaching people what God required of them, and He continually foretold His coming death and resurrection. And He did one more thing: He claimed to be God.

Because of Jesus' claim to be God, the leading religious people, along with the political powers of the day, passed an unjust sentence of death upon Him. Although He had never done anything wrong, He was beaten, mocked, and shamefully executed. When He died, it looked as if He had failed, but His death was part of God's plan from the very beginning.

Jesus' body was taken down from the cross and laid hastily in a rock tomb in a garden. After three days, some of His followers went to go properly care for His remains. But when they arrived, they discovered that He had risen from the dead. They spoke with Him, touched Him, and ate with Him. This is the story that we celebrate at Easter. After another forty days, He was taken back up into heaven, still in physical form, and His followers were told that He would return to earth in just the same way.

I mentioned that there were two things you need to believe to be a Christian. In addition to knowing you need more help than you or any other mere human could ever supply, you also need to believe that Jesus, the Christ, is the One who will supply that help and that if you come to Him, He will not turn His back on you. You don't need to understand much more than that. If you believe these truths, you will be welcomed by Him through His love, and you can know for certain that you have eternal life.

As you read these verses from the Bible, you can talk to God, as though He were sitting right beside you (after all, His presence is everywhere!). You can ask Him for help to understand. Remember, your help isn't based on your ability to perfectly understand, and it isn't based on anything you do. If you trust Him, He has promised to help you, and that's all you need to know for now.

All have sinned and fall short of the glory of God.
ROMANS 3:23

The wages of sin is death, but the free gift of God is eternal life in Christ Jesus our Lord.   ROMANS 6:23

While we were still weak, at the right time Christ died for the ungodly. For one will scarcely die for a righteous person—though perhaps for a good person one would dare even to die—but God shows his love for us in that while we were still sinners, Christ died for us.   ROMANS 5:6-8

For our sake [God] made him to be sin who knew
no sin, so that in him we might become the righteousness of God.   2 CORINTHIANS 5:21

If you confess with your mouth that Jesus is Lord
and believe in your heart that God raised him from
the dead, you will be saved. For with the heart
one believes and is justified, and with the mouth
one confesses and is saved. For the Scripture says,
"Everyone who believes in him will not be put to
shame." . . . The same Lord is Lord of all, bestowing
his riches on all who call on him. For "everyone who
calls on the name of the Lord will be saved."
ROMANS 10:9-13

[Jesus said,] "Whoever comes to me I will never cast
out."   JOHN 6:37

If anyone is in Christ, he is a new creation. The old
has passed away; behold, the new has come.
2 CORINTHIANS 5:17

[Jesus said,] "Come to me, all who labor and are
heavy laden, and I will give you rest. Take my yoke
upon you, and learn from me, for I am gentle and
lowly in heart, and you will find rest for your souls."
MATTHEW 11:28-29

There is therefore now no condemnation for those
who are in Christ Jesus.   ROMANS 8:1

If you'd like to, you might pray a prayer something like this:

Dear God,

I'll admit that I don't understand everything about this, but I do believe these two things: I need help, and You want to help me. I confess that I've pretty much ignored You my whole life, except when I was in trouble or just wanted to feel good about myself. I know I haven't loved You or my neighbor well, so it's true that I deserve to be punished, and I really do need help.

But I also believe that You've brought me here, right now, to read this page, because You are willing to help me. If I ask You for help, I know You won't send me away empty handed. I'm beginning to understand that You punished Your Son in my place and that, because of His sacrifice for me, I can have a relationship with You.

Father, please guide me to a good church and help me understand Your Word. I give my life to You and ask You to make me Yours.

In Jesus' name, amen.

In His kindness, Jesus established His church to encourage us and to help us understand and live out these two truths. If you know that you need help and you think Jesus is able to supply that help (or if you're still questioning but want to know more), please search out a good church in your area and begin to make relationships there. A good church is one that recognizes that we can't save ourselves by our own goodness and that only Jesus Christ (and no one else) can bring this salvation.

You can call around and ask about churches that meet these requirements, or you can go online and get a listing of churches in your area. Most churches have something called a "statement of faith" on their website, where you can get information about them. Mormons and Jehovah's Witnesses are not Christian churches, and they don't believe in the gospel (though they might tell you that they do), so you don't want to go there.

Finding a good church is sometimes quite a process, so don't be discouraged if you don't succeed right away. Keep trying, and keep believing that God will help you.

Another practice that will help you grow in this new life of faith is to begin reading what God has said about Himself and about us in His Word, the Bible. In the New Testament (the last one-third or so of the Bible), there are four Gospels, or narratives, about the life of Jesus. I recommend that you start with the first one, Matthew, and then work your way through the other three. I also recommend that you purchase a good modern translation (not a paraphrase), such as the English Standard Version.

If you've decided while reading this book that you want to follow Jesus, I would love to have you contact me through my website, www.elysefitzpatrick.com.

I trust that the Lord will continue to help you understand and become who He wants you to be: a person who has been so loved by Him that you're transformed in both your identity and your life.

SCRIPTURES FOR WEARY WOMEN

When You Think You've Messed Up Too Much to Be Accepted by God . . .

The LORD has taken away the judgments against you; he has cleared away your enemies.
ZEPHANIAH 3:15

God shows his love for us in that while we were still sinners, Christ died for us. Since, therefore, we have now been justified by his blood, much more shall we be saved by him from the wrath of God.
ROMANS 5:8-9

As one trespass led to condemnation for all men, so one act of righteousness leads to justification and life for all men. ROMANS 5:18

There is therefore now no condemnation for those who are in Christ Jesus. ROMANS 8:1

We know that a person is not justified by works of the law but through faith in Jesus Christ, so we also have believed in Christ Jesus, in order to be justified by faith in Christ and not by works of the law, because by works of the law no one will be justified. GALATIANS 2:16

In him we have redemption through his blood, the forgiveness of our trespasses, according to the riches of his grace. EPHESIANS 1:7

By a single offering [Jesus] has perfected for all time those who are being sanctified. HEBREWS 10:14

When You Are Tired of Striving to Make God Like You . . .

[The Lord] does not deal with us according to our sins,
  nor repay us according to our iniquities.
For as high as the heavens are above the earth,
  so great is his steadfast love toward those who fear
    him;
as far as the east is from the west,
  so far does he remove our transgressions from us.
PSALM 103:10-12

Now the righteousness of God has been manifested
apart from the law . . . the righteousness of God
through faith in Jesus Christ for all who believe.
ROMANS 3:21-22

To the one who works, his wages are not counted as a
gift but as his due. And to the one who does not work
but believes in him who justifies the ungodly, his faith
is counted as righteousness.   ROMANS 4:4-5

Who shall bring any charge against God's elect? It
is God who justifies. Who is to condemn? Christ
Jesus is the one who died—more than that, who was
raised—who is at the right hand of God, who indeed
is interceding for us.   ROMANS 8:33-34

In this is love, not that we have loved God but that
he loved us and sent his Son to be the propitiation
[the sacrifice that takes away wrath] for our sins.
I JOHN 4:10

When You Are Trying to Be Okay in Your Own Eyes . . .

You therefore must be perfect, as your heavenly
Father is perfect.   MATTHEW 5:48

[Jesus said,] "Do not think that I have come to abolish the Law or the Prophets; I have not come to
abolish them but to fulfill them."   MATTHEW 5:17

Being ignorant of the righteousness of God, and seeking to establish their own, they did not submit to God's righteousness. For Christ is the end of the law for righteousness to everyone who believes. ROMANS 10:3-4

We know that a person is not justified by works of the law but through faith in Jesus Christ . . . because by works of the law no one will be justified. GALATIANS 2:16

I have been crucified with Christ. It is no longer I who live, but Christ who lives in me . . . for if righteousness were through the law, then Christ died for no purpose. GALATIANS 2:20-21

O foolish Galatians! Who has bewitched you? . . . Let me ask you only this: Did you receive the Spirit by works of the law or by hearing with faith? Are you so foolish? Having begun by the Spirit, are you now being perfected by the flesh? GALATIANS 3:1-3

When the fullness of time had come, God sent forth his Son, born of woman, born under the law, to redeem those who were under the law, so that we might receive adoption as sons. GALATIANS 4:4-5

For freedom Christ has set us free; stand firm therefore, and do not submit again to a yoke of slavery. GALATIANS 5:1

When You Are Desperate for True Rest . . .

O God, you are my God; earnestly I seek you;
   my soul thirsts for you;
my flesh faints for you,
   as in a dry and weary land where there is no water. . . .

For you have been my help,
   and in the shadow of your wings I will sing for joy.
My soul clings to you;
   your right hand upholds me.
PSALM 63:1, 7-8

[The Lord says,] "I will satisfy the weary soul, and
every languishing soul I will replenish."
JEREMIAH 31:25

[Jesus said,] "Come to me, all who labor and are
heavy laden, and I will give you rest. Take my yoke
upon you, and learn from me, for I am gentle and
lowly in heart, and you will find rest for your souls.
For my yoke is easy, and my burden is light."
MATTHEW 11:28-30

On the last day of the feast, the great day, Jesus stood
up and cried out, "If anyone thirsts, let him come to
me and drink."   JOHN 7:37

We see that they were unable to enter [into rest]
because of unbelief.   HEBREWS 3:19

While the promise of entering his rest still stands, let us fear lest any of you should seem to have failed to reach it. . . . For whoever has entered God's rest has also rested from his works as God did from his.
HEBREWS 4:1, 10

Let us then with confidence draw near to the throne of grace, that we may receive mercy and find grace to help in time of need.   HEBREWS 4:16

Being made perfect, [Jesus] became the source of eternal salvation to all who obey him.   HEBREWS 5:9

ACKNOWLEDGMENTS

WHERE TO START in thanking those who made this book possible? I'll say right from the beginning that I won't remember everyone or say all that should be said. Please forgive me. It is impossible for me to give proper thanks to the many people who made this work feasible, who have taught, encouraged, prayed for, and blessed me in more ways than I can tell . . . but I will try.

I am thankful for all the "old dead guys" I've read who have formed my thought. I am thankful for all the not-so-old, not-yet-dead men and women who have taught me and opened my eyes to the truth about the good news and the ways the good news is to transform our lives. Here I'm thinking particularly of my dear friends Tullian Tchividjian, Justin Holcomb, Paul Tripp, and Iain and Barb Duguid. I am thankful for the ministry of the White Horse Inn, Issues Etc., KeyLife Network, and Westminster Seminary California and for the wonderful pastors and elders who have poured into my life over the years through sermons I've attended and accessed online.

I am thankful for my church, Valley Center Community, and particularly for my pastors and elders there: John Sale, David Wojnicki, Tony Suitor, Paul Benemen, Jon Walters,

Jason Smith, and my husband, Phil. I am thankful for my friends in the church who have prayed for me throughout this process and excused me from serving. I am thankful for our gospel community group, especially Margaret, Shannon, Kimm, Michele, Paula, Ilyse and all the guys, and for the ways you've prayed for me.

I am thankful for all my Facebook friends who have prayed for me, for all the messages I received through e-mail or Twitter letting me know you have brought me before His throne. Thank you.

I am also so very grateful for my dear lifelong BFFs, especially Julie, Donna, and Anita. Thank you for loving me and for continuing to pray.

I am particularly thankful for Resurgence Publishing, for John Weston, and for my new friends at Tyndale House, especially Stephanie Rische, editor extraordinaire. None of those connections could have been made, however, and this book would not have been written, without the gracious care, generous encouragement, and invaluable help of Pastor Mark Driscoll and the executive elders at Mars Hill. Thank you for all you do for the Lord and for your courage to stand for Him in this day. Thank you for loving women enough to want to speak truth, not put fluff or bricks into their lives. My thanks also goes to Hilary Tompkins, women's ministry leader at Mars Hill, for all the work she did to help me. Thank you for praying for me and for loving women the way you do. He sees.

And, of course, I am always indebted to my family for their love, prayer, and patience with me as I struggled with this project and walked around in zombie mode every day for months. Phil, as always, has been exceptionally kind to me, shoving food under the door and telling me, as he did when I was in labor with our kids, "You're almost there, honey," all the while hoping that the zombie didn't come lurching out of its chamber to bite him.

I have been blessed with three wonderful children who have wonderful spouses: James and Michelle, Cody and Jessica, and Joel and Ruth. Their continuous love and support mean more to me than I can say. My mother, Rosemary, and my brother, Rick, have prayed for me, and for that I'm thankful. And, of course, I'm so thankful for my darlings: Wesley, Hayden, Eowyn, Allie, Gabe, and Colin. May you all ever know the difference between the law and the gospel, and may the good news of what He has done impel zealous love in your lives for His glory. I am blessed.

NOTES

1 Metro-Goldwyn-Mayer, SLM Production Group, 1982.

2 Wayne Grudem, ed., *Biblical Foundations for Manhood and Womanhood* (Wheaton, IL: Crossway, 2002), 15.

3 For a fuller discussion of gender roles, see "Core Beliefs," the Council on Biblical Manhood and Womanhood, http://cbmw.org/core-beliefs.

4 Now before you begin to ask whether I've gone off the deep end and have become a quasi feminist, let me be very clear about the positions I hold on these issues: the New Testament proves that Jesus loved and related to many women who felt comfortable and welcomed by Him and that He appreciated their companionship as they traveled with Him and supported Him out of their means.

I believe that both men and women are equally created in the image of God. That means that I hold to ontological equality of the sexes.

I believe that both men and women are equally fallen and equally open to deception and sin. I hold to hamartiological equality of the sexes.

I believe that both men and women are equally called to repentance, faith, and new birth. I hold to soteriological equality of the sexes.

I believe that both men and women will be seated around the table at the marriage supper of the Lamb, where both males and females will be called the bride of Christ. I militate ferociously against any view of heaven whereby women will be sex slaves to meritorious men. I hold to eschatological equality of the sexes.

I believe that both men and women are equally gifted to fulfill the roles they have been called to. I believe in a pneumatological equality of the sexes.

I believe that God has established specific gender roles for men and women in the home and church that coincide with their creation design. In this I am complementarian; in other words, I believe that women were created to come alongside men and to be a complement to their creation design in the home and the church.

I militate ferociously against any view of women that demeans them, makes them chattel, enslaves them, abuses them, or harms them in any way as a function of the misogynistic lie that women have intrinsically less value than men. I'm especially opposed to the misguided presumption heard in some religious circles that the difficulties in the world are all Eve's fault. Isn't it just like Satan to tempt Eve to sin and then use her fall to shame and harm all of her daughters?

I militate strongly against any view of submission that insinuates that women are called to submit because they have less value or less innate ability to discern, or that submission must extend to every sphere of life, even if a woman is being asked to sin or compromise her conscience. I also militate against the notion that all women are supposed to submit to all men regardless of the relationship between them.

I'm thankful for the right to vote in both my church and my country.

I think that equal pay for equal work is proper and a great good, and I find it discouraging and distressing when women are paid less for the same work as men because somehow men need the money more or are more valuable.

I think that women should have the same property and civil rights as men in a free society like ours.

I think that abortion is a great evil that has not only slaughtered millions of infant girls and boys but also deeply wounded millions of women and men.

I believe that men have been ordained by God to lead their home and the church and that God has gifted women to help them in many ways. I also believe that women can and should assist men in their leadership by leading as they are asked to and able to.

I believe that women are gifted by God to work alongside male leaders in the church in many roles, including serving as deacons, fulfilling mercy ministries, teaching, participating in music ministry, evangelizing, and counseling. I believe that I am free to teach a mixed-gender audience in a conference format where other nonordained men and women are allowed to teach.

If you're really interested in what I believe about men's and women's roles, specifically in the home, see my book *Helper by Design* (Chicago: Moody Publishers, 2003).

While I do hold to the complementarian position, I hold this position loosely and am not willing to die on this hill, nor do I think that these positions are fundamental lines of demarcation between true and false believers. The salient point is trust in the efficacy of the life, death, and resurrection of Christ—and nothing else.

5 Dr. Barrs is referring to Ephesians 5; 1 Corinthians 11, 14; and 1 Timothy 2.

6 Melanie Benedict, "Seeing Women through God's Eyes," *ByFaith*, June 11, 2009, http://byfaithonline.com/seeing-women-through-gods-eyes (emphasis added).

7 Again, I'm not saying there's nothing good in these books. But there has been an overemphasis on these two passages in particular, and there needs to be a corrective.

8 I realize I am painting with a very broad brush. Some women in urban contexts or from certain denominations have not been forced into this mold, but the reality remains that in much of conservative evangelicalism, this is the general rule.

9 *ESV Study Bible* (Wheaton, IL: Crossway, 2008), note on Romans 16:1.

10 *ESV Gospel Transformation Bible* (Wheaton, IL: Crossway, 2013), study note on John 6:22-59.

11 Mark Driscoll, *A Call to Resurgence: Will Christianity Have a Funeral or a Future?* (Carol Stream, IL: Tyndale, 2013), 8.

12 Warner Bros., 2013. From IMDb.

13 Christian Smith with Melinda Lundquist Denton, *Soul Searching: The Religious and Spiritual Lives of American Teenagers* (2005; repr., New York: Oxford University Press, 2009).

14 In 1 Timothy 2:14 Paul does say that Eve was deceived first, but that deception was not because she had an inherent flaw because of the way God designed her. It is simply a statement that Eve was deceived and that her role as her husband's helper was thereby marred. The *ESV Study Bible* note on 1 Timothy 2:14 says that even though "Eve sinned first as a result of being deceived, Adam's sin was conscious and willful, with devastating consequences for the whole human race (see Romans 5:12)." If women should be precluded from studying doctrine because Eve was deceived, men should also be precluded because Adam was not deceived but was willfully disobedient.

15 Michka Assayas, *Bono: In Conversation with Michka Assayas* (New York: Riverhead Books, 2005), 205.

16 Dustin Kensrue, "It's Not Enough," *The Water and the Blood*, released September 30, 2013, Tower Records, 139th Broadway, compact disc.

17 In the Roman Catholic Church in the twelfth and thirteenth centuries, people believed they could lessen the amount of time they spent in purgatory for sins they'd committed (even though they'd been forgiven) by doing good deeds or giving money. This anti-gospel practice was one of the primary reasons for the Protestant Reformation. The focus of the Reformation was that people can't earn merit or make up for sins they've committed. Complete forgiveness must come by grace alone through faith alone in Christ alone. To try to add more work to Christ's perfect work was anathema to people like Martin Luther and John Calvin.

18 The book of Proverbs is intended to tell us generally how the universe works best. I've heard Mike Horton say that Solomon's proverbs tell us what direction the grain of the universe runs and that when we ignore that grain, we come up against trouble. In my words, we avoid splinters and things run more smoothly when we go with, rather than against, the grain.

19 Dennis Johnson, as quoted in my book *Helper by Design* (Chicago: Moody, 2003), 187. Dr. Johnson is a professor of practical theology at Westminster Seminary California. These notes were from a personal correspondence I had with him.

20 This is just one more reason women should be encouraged to study the Word and to read books that stretch them theologically. A basic study, either on your own or with other women, about the differing genres found in the Bible will do a lot to help you interpret what you are reading. For instance, knowing what type of literature Proverbs fits into will help you understand what you are reading and how it might apply to your life. I personally enjoy the *ESV Study Bible* and the study notes in the *ESV Gospel Transformation Bible*. I frequently refer to them when I'm trying to understand what the Lord might be saying to me through His Word.

21 According to the *ESV Study Bible* note, "The Hebrew word also covers causing human death through carelessness or negligence."

22 At this point, I'm not even going to opine about whether eating organic will make you healthier or not. I'll just go with the assumption.

23 Martin Luther, *Galatians*, Crossway Classic Commentaries (Wheaton, IL: Crossway Books, 1998), xxii.

24 Luther, *Galatians*, 177.

25 Luther, *Galatians*, 169.

26 *ESV Gospel Transformation Bible* (Wheaton, IL: Crossway, 2013), study note on John 4:16-26.

27 John T. Pless, *Handling the Word of Truth: Law and Gospel in the Church Today* (St. Louis: Concordia, 2004), e-book, location 180.

28 C. S. Lewis, *Christian Reflections* (Grand Rapids: Eerdmans, 1967), 14.

29 Dr. Art Lindsley, "C. S. Lewis on Humility (and Pride)," C. S. Lewis Institute, October 8, 2012, www.cslewisinstitute.org/C.S._Lewis_on _Humility_and_Pride. Accessed April 23, 2014.

30 John LaRosa, "Self-Improvement Market Has Unfilled Niches for Entrepreneurs," PRWeb, March 26, 2012, www.prweb.com/releases /2012/3/prweb9323729.htm.

31 Thanks to my son, Joel Fitzpatrick, for helping me understand this perspective on denying Christ in a sermon he preached at North City Presbyterian Church, Poway, California, on December 29, 2013.

32 Michael S. Heiser, "Glossary of Morpho-Syntactic Database Terminology" (Logos Bible Software, 2005).

33 *ESV Gospel Transformation Bible* (Wheaton, IL: Crossway, 2013), study note on John 14:6.

34 Ibid.

35 Ibid.

36 C. F. W. Walther, *The Proper Distinction between Law and Gospel* (St. Louis: Concordia, 1961).

37 Walter Marshall, *The Gospel Mystery of Sanctification: Growing in Holiness by Living in Union with Christ* (Eugene, OR: Wipf and Stock, 2005), 39–40.

38 Touchstone Pictures, 1988. From IMDb.

39 Katherine M. Harris, PhD, Sharon Larson, PhD, and Mark J. Edlund, MD, PhD, "Use of Prescription Psychiatric Drugs and Religious Service Attendance," *Psychiatric Services* 56, no. 4 (April 1, 2005): ps.psychiatryonline.org. In this study, people who did not attend church and people who were regular attenders had about the same usage level—about 30 percent of both groups used psychiatric prescription drugs. People who attended church only three to five times a year had the highest usage in the study (about 36 percent). For more on this topic, see my book, coauthored with Laura Hendrickson, *Will Medicine Stop the Pain?* (Chicago: Moody, 2006).

40 Walter Bauer, *A Greek-English Lexicon of the New Testament and Other Early Christian Literature*, 3rd ed., ed. and rev. Frederick William Danker (Chicago: University of Chicago Press, 2001), 444.

41 This saying is found in ancient Greek literature and Aesop's fables. It is not found anywhere in Scripture. And despite the fact that many Christians buy into this idea, it's completely anti-gospel. See this troubling study

about the level of confusion in the Christian community: George Barna and Mark Hatch, *Boiling Point: How Coming Cultural Shifts Will Change Your Life* (Ventura, CA: Regal, 2003), 173.

42 *ESV Study Bible* (Wheaton, IL: Crossway, 2008), note in the introduction to Isaiah, 1235.

43 Paul David Tripp, *Instruments in the Redeemer's Hands: People in Need of Change Helping People in Need of Change* (Phillipsburg, NJ: P & R Publishing, 2002), 35.

44 We can assume that Jesus functioned as a "single head of household" because at some point after His visit to Jerusalem at the age of twelve, His earthly father, Joseph, died. Joseph is never mentioned in any of the Gospels after that time, even though His mother, Mary, and His siblings are. By inference, we can assume that as the eldest son, Jesus took over the care of the home. In addition, when Jesus was dying on the cross, He gave the care of His mother over to His best friend (see John 19:26-27). Jesus would not have had to do so if Joseph had been alive.

45 See Deuteronomy 28.

46 Graeme Goldsworthy, *The Goldsworthy Trilogy: Gospel and Kingdom, Gospel and Wisdom, The Gospel in Revelation* (Waynesboro, GA: Paternoster Press, 2000), 174.

47 Timothy Keller with Kathy Keller, *The Meaning of Marriage: Facing the Complexities of Commitment with the Wisdom of God* (New York: Riverhead Books, 2011), 44.

48 Graeme Goldsworthy, *The Goldsworthy Trilogy: Gospel and Kingdom, Gospel and Wisdom, The Gospel in Revelation* (Waynesboro, GA: Paternoster Press, 2000), 174-75.

ABOUT THE AUTHOR

ELYSE FITZPATRICK has a master's in biblical counseling from Trinity Theological Seminary. She is the author of more than twenty books on daily living and the Christian life. A frequent speaker at women's conferences, she has been married for forty years and has three adult children and six really adorable grandchildren. Along with her husband, Phil, Elyse is a member of Valley Center Community Church, a Reformed congregation in the community of Valley Center, California.

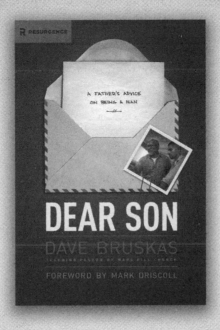